AGAINST THE WIND

Against the Wind

Douglas Sutherland

NEW ENGLISH LIBRARY
TIMES MIRROR

For Diana and Charles

First published in 1966 by William Heinemann Ltd.
© Douglas Sutherland 1966

*

FIRST NEL PAPERBACK EDITION MAY 1974

*

NEL Books are published by
New English Library Limited from Barnard's Inn, Holborn, London E.C.1.
Made and printed in Great Britain by Hunt Barnard Printing Ltd., Aylesbury, Bucks.

45001819 9

Yet, Freedom! yet thy banner, torn, but flying,
Streams like the thunder-storm *against* the wind.

Lord Byron

CONTENTS

ACKNOWLEDGEMENTS

I think I have acknowledged my indebtedness to other authors who have written about the Orkney Isles where the passages appear in the text. There are many others amongst my friends on the Island who have helped with suggestions and I would like to thank them collectively. In particular Bob Stevenson of the Bu told me many of the old stories which I have repeated, John Dennison, Ralph Fotheringhame, John Stevenson of Kirbister and Jackie Groat took part in many of the doings which I have described and Bunty Stevenson and her husband Willie helped me in many ways and with many kindnesses.

I would also like to thank Mr Macgillivray, the presiding genius at the County Library, Gerry Meyer, who edits *The Orcadian*, as well as Ernest Marwick and my cousin Bill Hutchison, both of whom read the typescript and made many helpful suggestions.

Finally my sincere thanks are due to Ian MacInnes, who volunteered to illustrate the book, for the delightful drawings which adorn it.

Douglas Sutherland

The author and the publishers are grateful to Messrs. Faber and Faber Ltd for permission to quote from Edwin Muir's poem 'Childhood', and to the Orcadian Office and Ernest W. Marwick Esq. for the material quoted on pages 16, 43 and 44.

Introduction

Some years ago I went to lunch in New York with the vice-president of a great corporation. He had his office thirty-eight floors above street level and we ate our meal there, looking down on the steel-and-glass canyon of Madison Avenue while the telephones rang and secretaries swished in and out of the room with letters and memoranda each marked with a different coloured tag according to its degree of urgency.

He was a quiet, middle-aged man who spoke with the pleasant drawl of an American from the Southern States and his job was to find each year the executives who were required to fill the top posts in the vast enterprise.

He told me that his problem was not the lack of potential talent but to persuade young men being groomed for stardom to accept a way of life which the statistics showed, put heavy odds on their being dead by the time they were sixty.

The thousands of rich American widows who pour each year by the busload across Europe are an eloquent testimony to a generation of successful businessmen who have retired in their prime and not lived to enjoy their material success. To combat the high mortality rate at an early age amongst their senior executives, many big corporations are now insisting that they take sabbaticals of a year or more in the belief that extended relief from the pressures of big business will prolong their life expectancy.

They have not, however, grasped the root of the matter. Prolonged work under high pressure, either physical or mental, does not break a man so utterly that all that is left of him is to crawl away into a corner and die. In fact there is plenty of evidence that quite the opposite is the case.

The trouble lies in the concept of what they are buying when they pay a man a salary. They believe that they are buying him body and soul for twenty-four hours a day, for three hundred and sixty-five days a year for as long as the contract lasts. No man can advance to the highest honours unless he accepts this concept – and not only for himself but for his wife as well. Even his children and his home and his friends must fit into the correct image. If his job is to sell soap powder, he must think it in his sleep and sing the television jingles at breakfast instead of saying the family prayers. To translate Greek elegiacs in his spare time instead of reading the latest market reports is an act of the basest treachery.

There is nothing wrong with this in itself as a contract between a buyer and a willing seller. It is only important that the seller should realise that the gold watch and the generous pension come gift-wrapped in an 'in memoriam' card. A man can retire in the fullest possession of all his faculties and sound in wind and limb but unless he has preserved something of himself he will be a remarkable man if he survives the amputation. Montaigne was right when he wrote, 'A man must keep for himself a small back room where he can be himself without reserve, for this is his only real freedom.'

We live in an age of pressures which close in on us from all sides. Everywhere there is struggle and in many cases the struggle remains a reality long after we have forgotten what we are striving after. It is an attitude which has been forged in the New World and is threatening to engulf the Old.

A man going to his work every day in a big city has not only the stresses of his job to contend with. To get there he has to compete for his seat in the train or his place in the bus queue and on the way home he must rejoin the battle. Even his lunch hour is part of the struggle. The executive with his business lunches is not more to be envied than his junior competing in the queue at the cafeteria.

Few homes today are a refuge from the outside world. The bulging briefcase is as much part of the furniture as the television set and leaning over the garden fence is the ever-present figure of Mr Jones whom everybody, by convention, must keep up with; and over everybody's shoulder is the sinister spectre of power politics in a nuclear age.

In the more leisurely days of the stage coach there was a saying that only bad news travels fast. In these days of instantaneous communications it is more than ever true. Every day we are assailed with the troubles of the world and hear little of the flowers in between. Unless we tend our flowers carefully, this modern world must become a cold barren place indeed.

In telling this story of a real island I am also telling the story of my own refuge where my own flowers grow. Although I left the island when I was quite young and only returned to it again at the onset of middle age, I have carried the memory of it with me to many parts of the world.

This book is then the affectionate biography of an island and a tribute to its changeless values in a world where everything is change.

Part One

Long time he lay upon the sunny hill,
    To his father's house below securely bound.
Far off the silent, changing sound was still,
    With the black islands lying thick around.

He saw each separate height, each vaguer hue,
    Where the massed islands rolled in mist away,
Though all ran together in his view
    He knew that unseen straits between them lay.

'Childhood' (*Edwin Muir*)

1. Childhood's Days

The Island lies off the north coast of Scotland. On one side it is buffeted by the great waves of the Atlantic rolling down from the Arctic Circle. On the other it is lapped by the waters of the North Sea. Between it and its neighbours the tides swirl dangerously and, when the wind blows, gigantic seas cut it off completely from the outside world.

It is irregularly shaped so that, although it measures seven miles from tip to farthest tip, there is nowhere which lies above a mile from the sea. In the summer it basks sleepily in the sunshine, the peat smoke from the hearths rising straight in the air. In the winter it seems to flatten out under the seas hurled against the cave-pitted cliffs and hold its breath as it is buffeted by hundred-mile-an-hour gales.

The Island's roots go down three thousand years in history and beyond that. The Picts once lived there until the Norsemen rowed out of the mists to possess them. The underground dwellings, brochs and burial-mounds which are scattered over the Island speak with different voices from the ages which have gone before. These relics of history and pre-history pose questions which baffle archaeologist and historian alike. Every now and again the ploughshare turns up another piece of the jigsaw but the main sites remain unexcavated, a fertile field of endeavour indeed for the generations of researchers to come.

Of all the northern isles it is in many ways the most emancipated and, at the same time, the most enigmatic. For over five hundred years its harbour was one of the most important fishing-ports in the northern seas, attracting fishing-boats from distant countries. Because its land is more fertile than any of its neighbours it has attracted settlers to a greater extent than any other, so that the origins of the Island families are diverse. Much that is Norse remains, obliterating the traces of earlier races and surviving the cultures of later years.

In each succeeding generation there are Islanders who leave home to seek their fortunes. A few return in their old age, but many more settle in the far corners of the world, for the blood of their colonist ancestors still runs strong in their veins.

On the Island the present lives comfortably with the past. Although the once prosperous fishing industry has now dwindled away and the population in the last hundred years has shrunk from over a thousand to less than half that number, it is still a vigorous, self-sufficient community. New ideas are superimposed on the old, and tradition goes hand-in-hand with progress.

My own first memories are of the Island and, although my family left while I was still young, they are deeply etched. In later years, at school, whenever the class was asked the definition of an isthmus, my hand was always the first in the air. My family's house was built on an isthmus so narrow that it was almost possible to throw a stone from one beach to the other. One one side there was only a road between the garden wall and the sea and, on the other, a narrow strip of land separated it from a sweep of sandy bay.

In my grandfather's day there had only been a small croft where he had come with his family of five boys to spend the summer months. For the rest of the year he had lived in a substantial, square house overlooking Kirkwall Bay on the Mainland, which is the name given to the largest island in the Orkney group. In his youth Grandfather had, like so many others, left the islands to seek his fortune in South Africa. He returned rich enough, at least by Island standards, and able to indulge in the luxury of what was rather grandly called a summer residence.

My father was his eldest son and had gone to Edinburgh University to study medicine. Then the 1914 war had come

18

along. By the time it was over, Grandfather had died and Father had married, and his health had suffered so badly from being gassed that he had given up any idea of taking his degree. Instead he decided to settle down on the Island and farm his lands there. His first step was to set about transforming the little 'summer residence' into a family house.

Father always had rather big ideas and the home he built was in keeping with them. Expert stonemasons were imported to dress the blocks of red sandstone hewn from the Island quarry, and elaborate gardens were laid out, surrounded by a fine stone wall. A garden on this scale was considered the height of luxury. Because of the violent gales any attempt to grow flowers could only be successful in the most sheltered positions. To achieve these he had great holes dug in the lawns and filled them with plants so that the garden consisted of a succession of rose-holes, tulip-holes and so on. It was, so far as I can remember, not a very successful experiment but a matter for wonder on the Island just the same.

Perhaps the greatest wonder of all, however, was the interior of the house. There are no trees on the Island, so that wood is a little used luxury which has to be imported all the way from Aberdeen. Instead of using fencing posts, fields were enclosed by stone dikes or simply by flat stones, set up with great labour edge on edge. The floors of the older houses were usually flagged and even the roofs made out of flat stones into which small, fixed panes of glass were chipped to give a little natural light.

In Father's house the floors were all of seasoned oak and the walls panelled, an unheard-of innovation. Even the ceilings were decorated with intricate patterns of wood so that the whole effect was of a baronial hall. Above the front door he had his coat of arms carved in stone and the door itself was made from a great, single slab of heavily studded oak which would have done credit to a medieval castle.

It was all built on one floor with what, to my brother Gordon and me as children, seemed miles of corridors opening off a large central hall. By and large it was quite the most remarkable house on the Island.

In his enthusiasm for home-making, Father scored a number of 'firsts'. He had, for example, the first wireless set on the Island and a racy, grey, open Sunbeam motor-car which he could never drive at much more than twenty miles an hour over the Island roads. The wireless set cost a hundred pounds and was a fantasy of gleaming valves and twisted wires. Because of the great distance from the transmitting station, immensely high masts, supported by guy-ropes, had to be erected on the lawn.

When the installation was complete, Father invited all the neighbours in to take turns at putting on the headphones and listening to the miraculous squeaks, whistles and grunts which came over clearly whenever the set was switched on. Occasionally very faint music could be heard in the background and even distant voices, although they were generally too far off to hear what was being said.

The voices never came any nearer and, with the passing of time, the novelty wore off. When one day the bull escaped and careered wildly into the garden, knocking down one of the masts, it was never put up again and the contraption was eventually put away for good in a cupboard.

In the summer the weather was idyllic; or so it seemed, for my childhood memories of week after week of blazing sunshine are not now confirmed by the older Islanders. Anyhow, whatever the weather, we spent all our time out-of-doors occupying ourselves with a hundred and one fascinating pursuits. We had a governess, Miss Johnstone, who had been a swimming champion picked to compete in the Olympic Games. While we played on the beach, she would swim for what appeared to be miles out to sea until all we could see of her was a white bathing cap, bobbing up and down like a tiny egg-shell in the waves.

Then there were the trips out to the headlands where we had picnics on the carpets of sea-pinks which covered one end of the Island. In other places the birds' nests were so close together on the ground that it was difficult to set a foot between them.

There was never much variation in our routine, but the routine itself was wholly satisfying, keeping us absorbed from getting up in the morning until the time came for reluctant bed.

Very occasionally, and as a great treat, we would be taken for a trip to Kirkwall on the biggest island. The boat never went direct to Kirkwall but would call first at other islands to drop off or pick up passengers and goods. These stops were often the occasion for some unexpected excitement.

Once a pig, which was being driven up the gangplank, squeezed under the rail and took a dramatic dive into the sea twenty feet below. My brother and I had often been told that a pig could not swim very far without cutting its throat with its own fore-trotters. Armed with this gory piece of information we watched with more than usual interest as the pig struck bravely out to sea. It was only recaptured after a stirring chase in a rowing-boat. Our sadness that its bid for freedom had failed was only matched by our disappointment at having our fascinating theory disproved.

Kirkwall was a town of ineffable delight. By comparison with the isolation of the Island it was all bustle and excitement. The narrow paved streets on which pedestrians, horse-drawn vehicles and cars all made their way together were lined with brightly-lit shop windows. In the harbour great ships lay at anchor bearing the names of faraway places like Aberdeen and even Leith; and, almost most exciting of all, up at the far end of the main street, sheltered by the buildings, there grew a tree! A tree was something so exotic in our experience that whenever we visited Kirkwall we could hardly wait to rush up the street to see if it was still there. It would not have surprised us if a panther had lurked amongst its branches waiting to pounce down on an unwary passer-by or if brightly plumage parrots had hopped from twig to twig.

My parents were very friendly with Mr and Mrs MacKay who kept the hotel which looked out over the harbour. After the shopping had been completed we would repair there to take tea. We were always impatient to finish the meal, for then we knew that the curtains would be drawn and a white sheet hung up above the fireplace while Mr MacKay got out his cinematograph machine to display the latest rolls of Mickey Mouse epics which were sent to him all the way from London. To us it was a far more fabulous invention than Father's wireless set and I can remember the details of Mickey Mouse's adventures with great clarity even today. Oddly enough I never saw another moving picture until I was about fourteen, long after we had left the Island. Then I was taken to see *Ben Hur* but did not find it nearly so impressive a performance.

The most exciting times on the Island were not during the quiet summer months but in the autumn and winter when the winds blew and life was lived to the almost constant accompaniment of the roaring of the sea.

After a night of gales, the wind would sometimes drop suddenly in the morning. Then we would make our way along the high-water mark on the sandy beach on the north side of the Island to discover the incredible variety of fish which had been hurled up out of the sea. Every few yards there would be a different species to examine. Great triangular skate with their long whip-like tails, quantities of halibut and vacant-looking

21

cod. Sometimes there would even be small sharks which would lie there for weeks until the birds had picked their bones clean, or tiny, chubby pilot fish, which accompany sharks wherever they go, feeding off what is left of their victims.

When there is a gale on the way, it is easy enough to recognise the signs. Long before the first sharp puffs riffle across the bay, the sheep give warning. At first the move to the low ground is leisured. They edge their way off the exposed headlands with casual nonchalance, nibbling as they go. Their gathering together seems almost accidental until, moved by a common impulse, they start down the narrow sheep tracks in single file, nose to tail, so that, viewed from a distance, they give the appearance of a continuous white tape writhing its way down the hillside.

Then the herring gulls start planing in from the Atlantic, trimming their wings to the freshening currents of air and spiralling down into the sheltered bays on the south side of the Island until the whole foreshore is clamorous with them. Other birds join them, splashing into the water beside the angry gulls, two by two, Noah's Ark fashion. Eider duck and mallard, and the little ringed plover with their urgent cheeky movements, oyster catchers, greenshanks and redshanks all driven by the same infallible instinct to shelter from the approaching storm.

Last of all come the mobbing skuas and the great black-backed gulls swinging in from their deep-water stations, all enmities forgotten in the face of the common danger.

One year the first storm came exceptionally early. It had been a blisteringly hot day and we were walking home with Father from an afternoon watching the birds swoop and dive around Rothiesholm Head. At the unmistakable signs that there was a big blow on the way, Father's pace became brisker and brisker. Then, as he remembered his new hen house, he broke into a jog-trot and we, with our shorter legs, had to run for all our worth to keep up with him.

The hen house had only been erected the day before and it now stood, with its complement of hens, out behind the cow byre without a single stake to hold it down, so that the first puff would certainly carry it out to sea.

Every storm produced its own catalogue of damage. There would be windows blown in and slates off the roofs and some-times quite substantial structures completely swept away. Everything that was movable had to be securely anchored to the ground to have any hope of survival.

As we raced past the next-door farmer's road end, I could

see his whole family hard at work forking their two remaining stacks into their barn. They were going at it like people possessed.

The wind started about tea time. Sudden gusts at first, coming from nowhere and dying away just as suddenly. By the time it was getting dark it was blowing steadily but in earnest. Too late we remembered that, in our hurry to get on with the business of the hen house, we had left the picnic basket sitting on the roof of the pigsty. When I was sent for it, it had gone, whirled no doubt out to sea where it would be now providing some surprised fish with an unexpectedly easy meal.

As a treat we had our supper in the grown-ups' sitting-room, huddling round the fire whilst we listened to the wind beating against the storm shutters and to the rising roar of the sea. There is an extraordinary exhilaration in the sounds of a storm when you are safely barricaded against it. It sharpens the senses so that the simplest action, such as crossing a room, becomes charged with drama. We started a game of Snakes and Ladders but we soon found that we were paying little attention to it, waiting for the next big gust to come before picking up the dice to throw again.

In the end we gave up playing altogether and just sat and listened. In my imagination I could see the great plumes of spray being thrown high over Lamb Head, and, although it was over two miles away, the boom of the waves as they hit the cliffs came clearly to us on the wind.

Miss Johnstone had a theory that every seventh gust was a stronger one, like a thing she had about every seventh wave being bigger than the rest. They never were, although we used to pretend to believe her. Now we started to count the gusts of wind and, surprisingly, it seemed to work out right. When an extra strong gust came, the whole house flinched and the paraffin lamp swayed on its hook on the ceiling so that the shadows danced on the wall and gave the feeling that everything was moving, as if on a ship.

After a time we found it difficult to sit still ourselves. The house was filled with ominous crackings and sudden bangs which sent Mother hurrying from room to room fearful that a shutter had been blown in or that some other disaster had befallen. Inexplicably, a saucepan fell off the wall in the scullery and clattered across the floor with so much noise that we really did think for a moment that part of the house had been carried away.

Father had lashed the chicken house down with two wires

23

stretched over the roof and fixed to pickets driven fully three feet into the ground. Even so he was worried that it would not hold.

In spite of voluble protests from Mother, who was quite convinced that he would be blown clean away – and what would we do then left literally fatherless in the storm? – he plunged out across the yard and came back to report that the pickets were lifting and that the hens would have to be evacuated to the safety of the kitchen.

To add to the perils of the night, the sea had now risen so high on the north side that the spray was whipping against the buildings and turning the sandy, dry soil in the yard into a sodden, salty mire.

It took six journeys to bring all the hens in to sit blinking in the kitchen and looking, if possible, even more anxious and neurotic than usual. Only the cock took vigorous action to evade capture, so he was left to the last in the true tradition of the captain and his ship. It was to prove his undoing. As Father stood poised to make the last dash across no-man's-land, he saw the whole hen house lifted twenty feet into the air and, turning over and over, disappear into the darkness.

When I awoke the next morning after the excitements of the previous night, the first thing that filtered through to me was the silence. It was breathlessly quiet and, peering out from under the bedclothes, I could see that the sun was shafting through the cracks in the shutters. The contrast with the holocaust of the night before was so dramatic that it was some time before I was conscious of the angry roaring of the sea. Even then it did not affect the quality of the silence which had settled so deeply on the house that it made even the dripping of the bathroom tap sound unnaturally loud.

Without waiting even to dress, we hurried out in our night clothes to look in awe at the mountainous waves now towering out in the bay. On the site of the hen house there was only a jagged rent in the earth where one picket had pulled out, causing the other wire to snap like a thread; and as we looked, we caught sight of what was left of it. It had been blown two hundred yards up the road and now lay, a mass of broken boards and twisted roofing felt, where a stone dike had stopped it crashing into the sea.

Perched on the topmost spar, arrogantly flapping his bedraggled wings, was our cock. As we watched, he threw back his head and crowed a proud defiance to the watery world. Even at the age of five, it struck me as an incredible and inspiriting moment.

It was after one of these early storms that we found our baby grey seal.

Because the tide was high and the seas made it dangerous, we had reluctantly forgone our usual walk round the bay. Instead we took the path inland to where the cemetery stands overlooking the south end of the Island.

The seal was lying behind a dike where the waves must have deposited it fully a hundred yards from the water's edge. It was sound asleep, exhausted by its ordeal but, when we went to pick it up, it opened its big, doe eyes and gazed at us with an expression more of languid curiosity than anything else.

To us nothing could have been more completely adorable than this little, white, fluffy bundle which looked as if, were it to grow another inch, it would burst out of its skin. It could only have been a few days old. Even so we were lucky that it was not in a pugnacious frame of mind. From later experience of young seals I was to learn that they can use their teeth at an early age and a bite even from a baby seal is most unpleasant.

On the other hand, of all mammals in the wild state, seals become the most quickly used to man. They suffer from an overweening curiosity so that, if you come upon them suddenly basking on the rocks, they will beat a hasty retreat to the sea only to bob up again in the water a few yards away to get a good look at the intruder.

We carried our find back in triumph to the house, taking it in turns to struggle along under its considerable weight, for a baby seal weighs about thirty pounds.

It was not greeted with the enthusiasm we expected. Father and Mother raised every manner of objection to our keeping it. The chief objection was that it would die and that if it did not die it would only become a nuisance about the place.

Our desolation at the thought of losing such a wonderful pet was so unrestrained that, in the end, we were allowed to keep it. Nor was it long before the matter of the seal's survival became a matter of the first concern to everyone in the house. Because seal's milk is very much richer than cow's all the creamiest milk was reserved for it. To this cod-liver oil was added whilst we all subsisted ungrudgingly on the skimmed milk that was left over.

At first the seal was allowed to live in the kitchen, where it

25

slept for most of the day lying stretched out on the stone flags, its flippers straight down by its side and its muzzle stretched out for all the world like an exhausted dog. When it was awake it would lie on its back and lift its head to gaze with obvious interest at anyone who came through the door and sometimes, to our great delight, scratch its head in a puzzled way with one flipper as if wondering what on earth it was doing on our kitchen floor.

This state of comatose acceptance did not last for very long. Within a few days it was pulling itself across the floor with its fore-flippers, poking its nose into everything and overturning the bread bin and the scrap bucket with the greatest regularity. Soon the kitchen began to look as if it were in a continual state of being spring-cleaned, with everything from the floor piled up on the shelves and tables.

Indeed, the constant cleaning of the kitchen floor was becoming something of a necessity for our efforts to teach it house manners were notably unsuccessful. Nor was it content for long to lie and wait to be fed from the baby's bottle which had been set aside for its exclusive use. When it felt hungry, which was pretty well constantly, it would bleat in exactly the same demanding way as a new-born lamb. Worse, sometimes tears would pour down its cheeks in the most heartrending fashion.

The ease with which seals apparently burst into tears has, in fact, nothing to do with their emotions. It is simply that, when on dry land, Nature has not fitted them with ducts to dispose of surplus eye liquid so that the water overflows down their cheeks and gives the impression that they are overcome with grief.

After the seal had been in the house for about a week, Father's initial opposition had been completely overcome, but there was a distinct hardening in the attitude of the female members of the household who were finding the almost complete usurpation of the kitchen a trifle inconvenient. Father, on the other hand, had in some way managed to get himself recognised as the greatest authority on the seal's welfare and it was in this capacity that he decreed one day that it should be given an opportunity of swimming. In consequence the bath was filled almost to overflowing and we were all paraded to admire and applaud Baby's debut in its natural element.

Although discussions on a suitable name went on continuously, no name for the new arrival was ever finally agreed upon. It may have been something to do with the fact that nobody

26

could decide for certain what sex it was or purely that we were sadly lacking in imagination, but the seal remained known as Baby the whole time it was with us. It was a name which became more and more incongruous as time went on.

Baby's reaction to water was not at all what we had imagined. Father held it over the bath whilst it sniffed nervously and the tears poured lugubriously down its cheeks. Then, as it was gently lowered into the water, it struggled like a panic-stricken kitten afraid of getting its fur wet. Finally, when it was let go free, it scrabbled wildly at the smooth sides of the bath in its efforts to escape from a watery grave, at the same time drenching everybody in the room with the frantic lashing of its tail, whilst itself becoming more and more water-logged.

When it was eventually rescued from this undignified predicament it eyed us all with such reproach that we came to the conclusion that we owned the only non-swimming seal in captivity.

Baby's popularity took a further turn for the worse when he started to shed his long silky coat. (I think Baby *must* have been a 'he'.) He had taken to shambling up and down the corridors and soon the carpets were literally white with hairs. It was the last straw. He was banished amid vigorous protests from those who did not have to sweep the carpets, and from now on spent his time in the hay barn. He submitted to this indignity with surprisingly good grace and would come and bang against the kitchen door with his nose whenever he was hungry. Later he changed his sleeping quarters of his own accord and took up residence, of all places, under the car in the shed which did duty as a garage.

After a period of looking comically piebald, he got his new dappled grey, short-haired coat and altered his method of progression from a laborious slither to a sort of walloping motion using his fore- and hind-flippers alternately. This, if it looked more ungainly, improved his speed considerably so that he could follow us round like a dog, giving vent to ecstatic grunts of pleasure whenever any of us appeared.

Soon, too, he got over his aversion to water and would come down to the shore with us to splash around happily in the rocky pools. Sometimes, when he was in a playful mood, he would chase a ball round and round the pool; at others he would simply float face downwards and inert with his head under water as if he were dead.

27

We were terrified, of course, that one day Baby would take to the open sea and we should never set eyes on him again. To prevent this we used to stand careful guard on the seaward side of the pools while he had his play-time, but eventually the inevitable happened.

Bored with watching Baby in one of his 'feigning dead' moods, we allowed our attention to be distracted by finding a more than usually large fish in another of the rocky pools. When we looked again, Baby was too near the sea edge for us to stop him. All we could do was watch, rooted to the spot, as with one final wriggle of ecstasy he plunged into the waves. A few moments later and he was diving and frolicking far out in the bay. It was the most dreadful moment of our young lives and that night I cried myself to sleep in an agony of remorse and self-reproach.

Next morning when we were sitting, miserable and red-eyed at the breakfast-table, there was a familiar rattle at the back door and there was Baby looking eagerly for his morning bottle as if nothing had happened. After that he went down to the sea every day, staying away for hours at a time but always returning to sleep under the car. He became less and less keen on his bottle until finally he gave it up altogether and became completely self-supporting on the fish he caught in the bay.

As winter turned to spring Baby spent longer hours in the sea, even joining the wild seals which came into the bay from time to time, but he always returned at night to sleep under the car. It seemed inevitable that, when the breeding season came round again, he would eventually go out to join his own kind on the sea-girt holms and leave us for ever. It was, however, not to be.

To add to our other joys, we had been given Shetland ponies on which we used to gallop wildly along the beach, whilst the ponies did their best to put us off their backs. There are no more capricious and mischievous animals than Shetland ponies. Despite their small size and butter-won't-melt-in-our-mouths expression they are up to every conceivable trick to achieve the discomfiture of their riders. Our tumbles were repeated but, with such a short distance to fall and the soft sand to fall on, they were of little consequence. When we did fall off, Gordon's pony would stand amiably by waiting to be remounted whilst mine, if I let go of the reins, would career madly off down the beach and it would take us hours to recapture it.

It was while we were engaged one morning as usual in the recapture of my pony that we heard a rifle shot and, on going to investigate, found Baby dead up against a rock with a bullet hole in his head. The mystery of who shot him was never solved and we were heartbroken for a long time afterwards.

Who can see the Green Earth any more
As she was by the sources of time?
Who imagines her fields as they lay
In the sunshine unworn by the plough?
Who think as they thought,
The tribes who then roamed on her breast,
Her vigorous sons?

'The Future' (Matthew Arnold)

2. History and Folk-Lore

Apart from our parents and Miss Johnstone there were several people who played important parts in our lives. Perhaps it was because there were so few people whom we saw regularly that they stand out clearly in my memory.

There was Sandy, the vanman, who came down our end of the Island twice a week. He sat perched up on the box of his van behind a heavy Clydesdale mare, cracking his whip, while the iron-banded wheels crunched on the gritty road so that we could hear him coming long before he hove into view round the bend by the garden gate.

When he opened the doors at the back of his van such a variety of pleasant smells emanated from the interior as to be quite overpowering. There were shelves of freshly baked bread and every imaginable variety of cake. There were great jars of flour and sago and rice; there was shoe polish and beeswax, mealie puddings and salted herring. Most exciting of all there was a drawer in which the sweets were kept, all mixed up together in such profusion that, had the choice been left entirely to Gordon and me, we would have been half the day deciding between the rival merits of straps of liquorice and sugar pigs, humbugs and chocolate cigars.

If he was in a good mood, which was almost always, Sandy would allow us to drive with him to the next farm and, as often as not, slip us a free bar of chocolate which we would be careful to consume before we got home again for fear it would count against the ration which Miss Johnstone would allow us after our midday meal each day.

We were very friendly with the people in the Bu farm, which was our nearest neighbour and where there was a big family. The youngest were about our own age and much of our spare time was spent in and out of each other's houses. It was a relationship which was not without a tinge of envy on my part for, where our house was built entirely on one floor, they had a fine sweep of staircase in theirs leading to mysterious rooms above to which we never penetrated. Edwin, who was about my age, told me that they only went up them when they went to bed and I could think of no more thrilling way of ending the day.

Most exciting of all our friends was Peter who lived in an isolated croft out on Rothiesholm Head where he farmed a few acres, painstakingly won back from the heather. Peter's face was the colour of old mahogany and his bushy eyebrows were bleached white with the sun and the sea spray, for, like all the Island crofters, he earned his living as much from the sea as from the land. He wore an old fisherman's cap which I never once saw him take off and he rolled his own cigarettes dextrously with one hand, a feat which never failed to excite my admiration and my brother's.

There was no greater joy for us than to be allowed to spend the afternoon with Peter as he went about his tasks and, if we were a nuisance trotting along behind him, he never showed it. Everything he did was carried out with leisurely efficiency, whether it was building the peat stack outside his back door or sitting cross-legged in his kitchen repairing the torn mesh of his lobster pots.

His lonely cabin by the seashore was filled with everything to charm the heart of a boy. He was a bachelor and, I suppose, set in his ways. Certainly there was a place for everything and everything was in its place – but what wonderful things they

32

were. There was a knife with a curved blade which was kept high above our reach on the mantelshelf and was so sharp that it would cut anything which was laid against it. Dimly seen on the rafters above were his sea rods, laid neatly side by side and, in a deeply recessed cupboard which smelled of wax, there were mysterious tins, each kept for a purpose and where he could lay his hands at once on anything he wanted from a screw nail to brandy-butter balls which I believe he kept specially for the times we came to visit him.

To go fishing with Peter was a considerable treat. Best of all was fishing from the shore, when we would have to clamber out on the slippery rocks to the edge of the sea where the waves splashed in a flurry of spray. We always set out when the tide was at its lowest ebb. Having got out to the farthest rocks we would then have to retreat step by step before the encroaching tide whilst Peter, the water swirling around his thigh waders, slung his weighted line rhythmically far out into the swell. When he hauled in a fish we used to scramble for the honour of unhooking it and transferring it to the safety of the fishing basket.

Perhaps the most remarkable thing about Peter was his ability as a story-teller. He told tales which fired the imagination. I do not remember ever having seen a book in his house but he knew all the history of the Island as recorded in the *Orkneyinga Saga* by heart. Every Orkney schoolboy is brought up on the *Saga* which tells the heroic stories of derring-do, of plot, and counter-plot, of the foul deeds and famous victories of the Norse Jarls in the days when the islands owed allegiance to the Norwegian throne.

The history of the northern isles is so different from the history of Scotland that perhaps I may be excused for a brief diversion to tell it.

Countless ages ago the islands must have been part of a much larger land mass with a totally different climate, for once it was thickly wooded. Although no trees will now grow, the peat diggers still come across great tree trunks preserved where they first fell in the boggy earth. Some measure as much as five feet across. Birch, beech, ash and fir were plentiful and even the silver fir which will not grow on Scottish soil but is common in Norway. It is difficult to believe, when one of these logs is unearthed that it lived before the history of the islands began.

In those days deer and wild boar roamed the land; their antlers and tusks were still occasionally unearthed. Both died out long

3

ago although an experiment in the last century to reintroduce deer was so successful that they had to be destroyed again because of the damage they did to the crops.

The remarkable preservative qualities of the peat have been responsible for some strange discoveries. Not the least of them was when a crofter, digging his peats for the winter, unearthed the body of a young girl fully dressed and so perfectly preserved that she might have only recently been buried. Careful research identified her as the victim of an unsolved murder which had taken place 280 years earlier.

Long after much of the land had sunk again into the sea the Island was inhabited by the Picts – a remote and mysterious race about whom very little is known. The ubiquitous Phoenicians sailed from the warm shores of the Mediterranean to do business with them and Agricola must have seen them when he sailed northwards with his fleet to discover the ends of the earth. What he saw evidently satisfied him that his quest was completed. 'There Nature ends,' wrote a Roman chronicler, and Agricola, believing it so, christened the islands Ultima Thule – the end of the world.

St Columba's missionary monks later came to settle choosing the smallest islands on which to live as hermits. On most of these little islands traces of the hermit monks remain.

Here is one of the oldest mysteries of the imperfectly known history of the islands. There is ample evidence in the Pictish burial-grounds and in the numerous fortified brochs which surround the shores, that the islands once supported a large and vigorous population presumably ready and able to fight to defend what they held. And even before the Picts, reaching back into the mists of time, is the evidence of the great standing stones and circles, more imposing in their stark loneliness even than the monoliths of Stonehenge.

A thousand years ago, when the Vikings poured across the sea to conquer Normandy and to pillage and plunder the coasts of England and Scotland, they met with the most vigorous resistance. Only in the northern isles it would seem they met with little opposition. In the great Sagas in which the Vikings delighted in telling the story of their conquests, there is a single passing mention of their struggles to gain a foothold. The population were either not warlike enough to resist the invaders or they had already fled in the face of goodness knows what dangers.

The *Orkneyinga Saga* tells the story of the years when the

Vikings were overlords of the islands, owing allegiance not to Scotland but to Norway. The islands were subject to Norse rule from some time in the eighth or ninth centuries until as late as 1468 when they were pledged by King Christian of Denmark and Norway to James III of Scotland as part of the marriage settlement when James married his daughter Margaret.

This pledging of the islands to the Scottish King is still looked upon as a somewhat doubtful expedient by the islanders. This is what happened.

When the marriage was arranged between James and Margaret of Norway her dowry was set at 60,000 florins (about £45,000). In return, upon marriage, she was to be granted the palaces of Linlithgow and Doune and a third of the property and revenue of the Scottish crown. In the event, the impoverished King Christian could not raise anything like the money required. It was then agreed that he should pay only 10,000 crowns in cash and pledge the Orkney Isles, on which Scotland had already cast greedy eyes, for the balance of the money.

Even then he could not raise the ready cash and the following year it was agreed to accept only 2,000 crowns while Christian calmly threw in the Shetland Isles for the balance of 8,000.

The pledging was not, however unconditional. If James predeceased Margaret she was to have the option of returning to Norway and being paid 120,000 crowns for giving up her Scottish properties, out of which money the Orkney and Shetland Isles were to be redeemed at par – or they could be redeemed at any time for 58,000 crowns if Norway could find the money. And that is how the situation stands to this day! The fact that they were quietly annexed to the Scottish Crown by an Act of the Scottish Parliament in 1471 makes not the slightest difference. It was an illegal Act as, in fact, Christian's action in pledging the isles in the first place was probably illegal. As late as 1667 Norway's right to redeem the islands was fully recognised by the Treaty of Breda.

There was one further important condition accepted by Scotland at the time of the pledging. This was that the islanders should be allowed to continue to live under Norse law and not be subject to Scottish law on taxes and tenure of land. Needless to say the Scots were quick to forget their promises about taxes, but vestiges of the old Norse law with regard to what is known as udal land still exist, and this has proved the downfall of many a smart city lawyer from the south.

A udaller – a man who owns udal land – is a kind of peasant

nobleman such as never existed in England and Scotland under feudal law. Udal law is, in fact, the very antithesis of feudal law. A udaller is in every respect a freeholder, holding his land inalienably for himself and his heirs, and without any requirement of service or payment to any superior including the Monarch, who is only his equal at law. Even today there are islanders who like to argue that there are udallers who are freeholders in this sense but, alas, there are no real grounds for the romantic notion. However several peculiarities of udal law are still observed. One of them is that whereas under British law, the land between high-water mark and low-water mark belongs to the Crown, under udal law it belongs to the udaller.

On the islands this is vitally important land providing valuable grazing for sheep and giving the right to collect tangle, a type of seaweed used in various manufacturing processes. The grazing rights may appear negligible but they are, in fact, extremely important. So thrifty are the farmers that until recently they would even lower their sheep over the side of a cliff to take advantage of the grazing on the small, nearly inaccessible patches of grass growing on the cliff face. On the island of North Ronaldsay the grazing is totally enclosed by a wall, the purpose of which is not to keep the sheep enclosed but to exclude them from the rich pastures inland and force them to feed off the seaweed on the foreshore. These seaweed-fed sheep have so adapted themselves to their diet that they will die if deprived of it and forced to feed only on grass. In fact the North Ronaldsay sheep have almost developed into a breed of their own. When shorn of their wool they are little bigger than a large hare but the wool itself is of extraordinarily fine texture and the mutton they produce far superior to any other.

During the last war the Admiralty built a substantial jetty on one of the outlying islands. After the war they tried to claim rent from the owner of the island for the right to use the jetty. The lawyer for the owner pointed out that the jetty was built on udal land and should never have been built in the first place without the permission of the owner. A surprised Admiralty soon discovered that not only were they not entitled to any rent but that, under udal law, they owed the udaller rent for having put it there.

The islanders are steeped in their Norse ancestry but it is not generally so well understood farther south. It has resulted in many curious situations. A distant Department of Education in London for many years gave a special grant for the benefit of teachers in the Island schools who could speak Gaelic. Gaelic is of course only spoken in the Highland counties and in the Western Isles. In the Northern Isles the root language is Norse and a Gaelic teacher would be an oddity indeed.

The same remote authority joined the Orkney Isles with Banffshire to form one school inspector's district after, no doubt, a glance at a school atlas which showed the islands boxed in by a square arbitrarily placed somewhere in the Moray Firth. This practice of cartographers of moving the islands from their rightful place off the northernmost tip of Scotland to some convenient place in the North Sea farther down the coast is apt to cause confusion even amongst otherwise well-informed people.

Peter loved to re-tell the stories of the Norse Jarls. He always used to start his stories with 'Lang afore your faither an' me was born . . . ' which had the effect of making us believe that both Father and Peter were incredibly old and wise and at the same time placing the events he described as somewhere just before the Great War. This sense of timelessness is typical of the islanders. When one of them says 'That is were the old monastery used to stand' it is as if it were yesterday instead of a thousand years ago when it fell into disuse.

Today I have only to turn the pages of the *Orkneyinga Saga* to hear Peter's deep voice telling the stories and to see again the simple expressive gestures of the born story-teller.

The names of the heroes were almost as marvellous as the tales themselves. There was Erik Bloodaxe, the exiled King of Norway who was killed in a raid against England, and there was Thorfinn Skull-Cleaver who died rather disappointingly in his bed and lies buried, according to Peter, on South Ronald-say 'chust aboot where my Auntie Jessie's hoose is'. There was Sigtrygg Silkybeard, King of Dublin, who managed to get the Orkney Jarls involved in his efforts to overthrow the famed Brian Boru of Ireland which led to Earl Sigurd the Stout meeting his death at the Battle of Clontarf.

Another Sigurd was the first Earl of Orkney and he came to his death in a remarkable way which throws a light on the savagery of the times. Sigurd conducted a long series of raids against the Scottish Earl Maelbrigte until a meeting was finally agreed upon to discuss peace terms. It was also agreed that, at the meeting, each earl should only be accompanied by a body-guard of forty men. Sigurd did not altogether trust Maelbrigte so he arrived at the place appointed for the parley with a body-

37

guard of forty horses but took the precaution of mounting two men on each horse. The peace talks broke down and the opposing sides set about each other. With two Norsemen to every Scot it was not surprising that Maelbrigte's men were overwhelmed.

Riding home in triumph, with the head of his enemy dangling from the pommel of his saddle, Sigurd put spurs to his pony and in doing so drove one of Maelbrigte's protruding front teeth into his knee. The injury gave him blood poisoning from which he died. 'An' sarve him richt too,' Peter would add, for once taking the side of the despised Scots.

Another of his favourite stories was of the second great Orkney earl, Torf Einar, who, some say, got his name from the fact that he was supposed to have introduced the practice of using turf or peat as fuel for the island fires. Einar's father was slain in Norway by King Harald's son, Halfdan Highleg. The King was furious and, to escape his wrath, Halfdan fled to Orkney, which proved to be a case of out of the frying pan into the fire. There he had Torf to reckon with, who first of all defeated him in battle and then, to exact personal vengeance, pursued him from island to island.

He finally caught up with him on North Ronaldsay, the most remote of all the Orkney Isles. Scanning the bare island from the prow of his longboat, Einar suddenly exclaimed, 'I see something – sometimes standing up, sometimes lying down. It is either a bird or a man and we must go and see.' It proved to be the exhausted Halfdan who was at once slain and the blood eagle carved on his back by cutting the ribs from the spine and tearing out the lungs. Then the remains were sacrificed to Odin in gratitude that revenge had been granted.

As for Torf Einar, he, as all heroes should, lived happily ever after and his descendants continued to rule the islands for another three hundred years.

Not all Peter's stories had to do with the brave days of the Vikings. He had two other favourite subjects – the excisemen and the press-gang. We might be out in his boat looking for a lobster pot when he would suddenly lay on his oars and point to a cave in the cliff face. 'See yon cave?' he would say. 'Weel thon's where Davy Flett hid from the press-gang when they were after him chust a few years back.' Then he would sit back and tell us the tale as if it had happened yesterday instead of maybe over a hundred years ago. Indeed, when we were children, there were old men on the Island who could have told the tales of the press-gang days as they had been told to them by men who had lived in those times, so they were not all that remote. In a closely-knit, isolated community like the Island the stories were remembered and retold with all the clarity of actual experience.

Because they were seafaring people, the islanders were in great demand for pressing into the Navy and the press-gang officers used to lie in wait for the boats returning from the fishing grounds to claim their victims. All manner of devices were resorted to in order to avoid falling into their clutches, and many of the houses had the equivalent of a priest-hole which the able-bodied men of the house used as a hiding place.

There was one old man on the Island who is remembered because, whenever the press-gang was about, he would rush down to the beach and, placing his legs across one great stone, would hold another aloft and threaten to crush his legs if the press-gang constables attempted to lay a hand on him. As he was far above the age to be useful as a conscript, he is remembered with amusement but, for the most part, the press-ganging was a serious and grim business for it often meant the removal of the bread-winner of the family.

Many of the men who knew their names to be on the press-gang list took to the rocky cliffs where they lived like animals until the danger was past. A great many of the best-remembered stories have happy endings, with the hero evading capture and living on for many years to tell the tale to his children and his children's children. These stories are remembered with as much delight as the many stories of the local sport of evading the gaugers.

The gaugers were the excise officials whose job it was to stop the smuggling-in of French brandy as well as to prevent the manufacture of illicit spirits. It was felt by the authorities, quite rightly as it turned out, that any attempt to enforce the Excise Act in the far north would prove ineffective. It was therefore laid down for the islands that two persons should be selected from each parish as fit people to operate stills, for which right they were required to pay twenty shillings duty on each gallon produced. In fact the operation of illegal stills remained widespread and the amount of duty collected from legitimate manufacture was negligible.

The job of the gaugers was made the more difficult by the enthusiasm with which all the islanders, from the magistrates downwards, entered into the business of evading the law. Frequently, when making an unexpected raid, the gaugers would see a guilty-looking islander making off across the fields, staggering under the weight of a large sack, which they would at once assume to contain malt. The runner would lure them farther and farther on, in the same way that a bird by pretending to be wounded attempts to draw attention away from its nest. When the panting excisemen finally caught up with him the sack would be found to contain nothing but a featherweight load of chaff. In the meantime all the guilty evidence would have been removed.

Smuggling was considered a proper traffic for the town councillors and the wealthy merchants of Kirkwall and, with the islanders' enthusiastic support, they made a good thing of it. Finally the law was altered to give the farmers the right to brew their own ale under licence. Although the system continued to be subject to abuse it did have the effect of killing the trade of the full-time smugglers.

Like most of the crofters on the Island, Peter always brewed his own ale and I suspect made some of the 'real stuff' as well. I heard many years afterwards that he had the reputation of being one of the hardest drinkers on the Island and that when the drink was in him everyone stepped warily for he had a quick temper and the strength of ten men.

We knew nothing of that of course and, supposing we had, it would have made no difference. One's childhood heroes are never allowed to have feet of clay.

Another character on the Island who made a big impression on us as children, although for rather different reasons from the others, was Maggie.

The thing about Maggie was that she was a witch. She too lived alone by the sea in a little croft which she worked herself. That is to say that she was always to be seen pottering around her house, occupied with some task or another, but the heavy work on the croft like the ploughing or the harvest was always done for her by one of her neighbours. Because of her reputation her neighbours were unwilling to refuse her any favours she asked, for it was well known that she could make things quite unpleasant for anyone who dared to thwart her. The misfortune which befell Deedie Finlay was a case in point.

Deedie had the farm next door to Maggie and in consequence bore the brunt of most of her requests for assistance. One September when the harvest came round, Maggie, as usual, asked for the loan of Deedie's binder and two men to help her get her strip cut. Deedie himself was behindhand that year so he said that he would willingly lend her what she wanted but that it would have to wait until he had finished his own harvest. Next day, as Deedie's cart was going past Maggie's road end, to his great inconvenience the axle seized up and the cart would not move backwards or forwards. Maggie got her corn patch cut for her that afternoon.

Knowing her reputation, whenever we passed by Maggie's croft we were in a perfect panic lest she should see us and cast some kind of a spell over us, for certainly she looked every bit a witch.

It happened one day that I had stayed rather too late clambering amongst the rocks and was hurrying home so as not to be late for lunch when, greatly daring, I decided to take the short cut past Maggie's croft. To my consternation as I passed her garden wall I saw that she was out digging her potatoes. Hardly daring to breathe I kept on my way until, when I drew level with her, she lifted her head and remarked in the most matter-of-fact way that it was a warm kind of a day. I took one look at her toothless mouth and the grey locks straggling from under the shawl which she always wore about her head and, mumbling something, took to my heels and ran. Nor did I stop until I had got safely inside our front gate. In fact I believe now that Maggie was a completely harmless old woman but there is no doubt that her mother before her had real powers as a witch.

Her name was Betty and she is still remembered on the Island for her spell weaving. Our neighbours at the Bu farm had good reason for believing in her powers. One evening they were churning their milk in the kitchen at the Bu to make butter but, no matter how hard they churned, no butter would come. It was after they had been about their fruitless task for some time that one of the serving girls remarked that they must have offended old Betty in some way and she had 'taken the profit' on their butter, which is the Island way of saying that it had been bewitched.

The only thing to do, the maid told them, was for someone to creep into Betty's byre at dead of night and take away some of the milk from Betty's cow. If this could be achieved and the milk tipped into the churn, all would be well. Greatly daring, the maid herself said she would go and milk Betty's cow if one of the family would come with her to stand guard.

The task was successfully accomplished and, when the milk was added to the churn, it yielded up a greater amount of butter than ever before.

Next morning Betty at once detected what had happened.

41

'Whoever did last night's work,' she declared, 'will do no more work for a six-month.' At once the serving maid's arm went stiff and she lost the use of it until six months were passed.

I am aware that, in telling this story, I am laying myself open to ridicule. I cannot help that. The facts are well known to many people on the Island the girl who took the leading part in the exploit was alive until three years ago to tell the story herself.

The belief in witchcraft is deep-seated in the northern isles. There are probably few islanders today who would admit to believing in the supernatural but, equally, there are few who would categorically deny its possibility out of hand. In the days of the witch hunts, in which Scotland took a leading part, the islands did not lag far behind. Although the old witches were generally identified with evil doings, there were many who went to the stake for nothing more than effecting 'miraculous' cures or for acts of second sight. Many more, of course, met their fate because of some private spite on the part of the informer.

One of the most renowned witches in the islands was Granny Rendall. She lived in the seventeenth century and was generally known as the Spitting Witch from her habit of spitting over her shoulder when she had some more than usually weighty information to impart to those who came to her to have their fortunes told. She was either a good or a lucky fortune-teller, setting many a young girl's fear at rest by assuring her that her long-absent sailor lover would soon return safely to port.

It was inevitable that Granny Rendall should be dubbed a witch and equally inevitable that any natural misfortune which might occur, such as the sudden death of a cow or a poor crop of corn, should be laid at her door.

One of her chief enemies was a local farmer, Gilbert Sandie. By a strange twist of fate, Sandie's young son formed a great affection for Granny Rendall and was for ever to be found at her cottage, despite the threats and admonitions of his father.

One day the boy fell dangerously ill and it was soon evident that he was dying. Every day, as he grew weaker, he begged that Granny Rendall be allowed to visit him. Eventually the distraught father reluctantly agreed and she was sent for. For hours she remained by the boy's bedside, play-acting to keep him amused and nursing him with all the skill she possessed.

In spite of her care, the boy died but Gilbert Sandie was so impressed by the woman's obvious goodness that, when she was later arraigned on some other charge for witchcraft, he appeared to give evidence on her behalf. Unfortunately his testimony did more harm than good for the accused. His former antagonism was well known and the superstitious jurors decided that his change of heart could only mean that he was bewitched.

Granny Rendall was condemned to be worried at the stake and her body burned to ashes. Gilbert Sandie walked with her to the stake to comfort her in her ordeal. It was the witch who, in the end, did the comforting. As they placed the noose around her neck she leant forward and confided to him: 'Don't worry. Our wee lamb came and kissed me as he promised. I can see him now beckoning to me. He will do as much for you when you are nearing the end of your journey in this vale of tears.'

Our Island was famed amongst its neighbours for being the home of the Queen of all the witches and the witches' chair, fashioned out of rock and from which she was supposed to have held Court, is still a local landmark.

The Island also has the unenviable reputation of being one of the last places where a witch was done to death. She lived by the Muckle Water in the centre of the Island and there is no record of what heinous crimes she was held to be guilty of. There were no local courts on the islands and justice was apt to be summary. In this case the poor old woman was led out to the headland of Huip and there beaten to death with corn-flails. The islanders ensured God's blessing for their action by first dipping their flails in holy water.

Walter Traill Dennison, the famous Orkney historian of the last century, has recorded for posterity the procedure to be followed by anyone who wishes to obtain the powers of witchcraft. Here it is as it was told to him by an old woman who admitted to being a non-practising witch:*

'The person wishing to obtain the witch's knowledge must go down to the seashore at midnight, must, as she goes, turn three times against the course of the sun, must lie down flat on her back with her head to the south and on ground beween the lines of high and low water. She must grasp a stone in each hand, have a stone at each side of the foot, a stone at her head, a flat stone on her chest and another over her heart; and must lie with arms and legs stretched out. She will then shut her eyes, and slowly repeat the following Incantation:

> O, Mester King o' a' that's ill,
> Come fill me wi' the warlock skill,

*Quoted in Ernest Marwick's *Anthology of Orkney Verse*. (The Orcadian Office, 1949.)

An' I sall serve wi' all me will.
Trow tak' me gin I sinno!
Trow tak' me gin I winno!
Trow tak' me whin I cinno!
Come tak' me noo, an' tak' me a',
Tak lights and liver, pluck an' ga',
Tak' me, tak' me noo I say,
Fae de how o' de head tae de tip of de tae;
Tak' a' dat's in an oot o' me,
Tak' hide an' hair an' a' tae thee
Tak' hert an' harns, flesh, bleud an' buns,
Tak' a' atween de seven stuns.
In de name o' de muckle, black Wallawa!

The person must lie quiet for a little time after repeating the Incantation. Then, opening her eyes, she should turn on her left side, arise and fling the stones used in the operation into the sea. Each stone must be thrown singly; and with the throwing of each certain maledictions were to be said . . . '

What the maledictions were, the old woman would not say. Probably because they were too shocking to repeat!

Much more attractive than the grisly tales of witchcraft amongst the islands are the folk-lore tales of the little men who live in enchanted mounds on land or in a strange country under the sea. This belief in a race of little men is common to most island folk, and they are the direct ancestors of the gremlins invented by the Air Force during the last war as a way of accounting for any unexpected misfortune.

Although the little men could on occasions be kind and helpful, they were usually noted for spiteful little actions, such as turning the milk sour, and even such major misdemeanours as taking a baby from its cot and leaving a changeling in its place.

The land dwellers were known as hillie-trows and their places of residence were well known. Few would dare to pass them after sun-down and as recently as a hundred years ago it was usual on certain nights for the islanders to turn out in force and, by dint of making as much noise as they could, to drive the hillie-trows underground.

On certain nights the little folk came out to dance. A typical story of what happened to people who set eyes on them is of the farmer who, after a night of celebration, was returning to his farm one spring night. Emboldened by drink he took the short cut past the home of the hillie-trows. No sooner did he set eyes on their mound than he saw that they were all out dancing to music so irresistible that he could not stop himself from joining in. Leaping into the circle of dancers he footed it with the best of them, never drawing breath until quite suddenly the music stopped and he found himself alone again. It was only when he got home that he found that the harvest was in full swing and realised that his dancing had lasted for six months.

Much the same sort of tales are told about the Selkie-folk, which is the name given to the under-sea dwellers. They, too, occasionally came ashore to dance, shedding the seal skins which they habitually wore in their underwater world.

One of the best known of the stories about them and one which used to be told to us around the fireside on the long winter evenings, also concerns a farmer who early one morning came across them on the seashore dancing to unearthly music. Seeing their skins cast aside on a near-by rock, he crept forward and stole one of them when none of the dancers was looking. Thus, when dawn broke and the time had come for them to return again to the sea, there was one beautiful Selkie-maiden without the means of escape.

She was so lovely and of such a sweet nature that the farmer fell in love with her and she with him. They married and lived together for many years, and she bore him several handsome children.

Only on the nights when the Selkie-folk came ashore to dance was she restless, for, happy though she was, the enchantment of the land beneath the sea never completely left her. One night when the farmer was away from home to attend a market on the Mainland, she was wandering through the house with the distant music of the Selkie-folk in her ears when she came upon her seal skin where the farmer had hidden it deep in a cupboard. When he returned it was to find his wife had gone, reclaimed by her own people. Occasionally when the farmer was away from home she would return to see her children before disappearing again beneath the waves. As for the farmer, he never set eyes on her again.

Another legend is of the islands of the Fin-men which have a habit of appearing and disappearing in the mists; which is, in fact, what the real islands do. The Fin-men were a different breed from the Selkie-folk. Their women started life as mermaids and the men had a great knowledge of sorcery and magic as well as being formidable performers with an oar. It was said that it only took a Fin-man seven strokes to pass from Orkney to Norway.

One of the islands of the Fin-men used to be Eynhallow which lies close to the Mainland and which is cut off by the most terrifying rip-tides.

Eynhallow fair, Eynhallow free,
Eynhallow stands in the middle of the sea;
With a roaring roost on either side,
Eynhallow stands in the middle of the tide.

So runs the old Island rhyme about the Holy Isle. In legend Eynhallow was a vanishing island, but it was said that if any man who saw the island on one of its brief appearances were to hold steel in his hand and row towards it without once taking his eyes from it and gain a foothold upon it, he would win it for ever from the Fin-men who held it in thrall. Many perished in the attempt before the island was finally won, to stand where you can now see it, amidst the roaring tides.

There was one distinguished Moderator of the Church of Scotland who had a house which looked over the water to the island. He was once asked teasingly by a friend if he believed the story of the island. 'I never go up the stair of my house without pausing on the landing to peep through the window to see if Eynhallow is still there,' he replied solemnly.

If you, like the Moderator, are not so lost to romance as to disbelieve the story of Eynhallow, perhaps you will also believe in the island of Heather-Blether, for this is the real home of the Fin-men. It too is supposed to rise from time to time, green and fertile, from the waves and, if there is no one living who has actually seen it, there are plenty who have heard tell of it and that is surely good enough.

I would just like to add one more story which Peter used to tell us and which I had never heard of anywhere else until the other day. It concerns the barnacle goose which is a winter visitor to the Island. It nests on remote islands in the Arctic Circle but in the old days, Peter assured us, men believed its origins to be miraculous. It was said that on the Orkney Islands there was a barnacle tree which grew by the seashore. Instead of flowers it grew white shells on its branches and each shell contained a tiny living creature. When it shed its strange blossom, the shells fell into the sea and, the moment they touched the water, each shell turned into barnacle goose.

I always thought the story of the barnacle tree to be the

46

product of Peter's remarkable imagination until I came across the story retold in *The Times*. It read:

'The myth of the Barnacle Tree goes back to the remote ages and is referred to by many early authors. A paper on the subject was even read to the Royal Society in 1677 and afterwards published. Pope Pius II was anxious to see the Goose Tree when on his travels but was told it only grew in the Orkney Isles. . . . Even when their nesting place was discovered by Dutch explorers, egg laying was, for many years, regarded only as an alternative form of origination.'

Where Peter first heard all the stories he had to tell, I cannot imagine, but his telling of them certainly made our childhood more golden.

When I returned to the Island many years after, he was one of the first people I asked about. Then I learned that he had gone down with his boat in an Arctic convoy during the last war and, when I visited his croft, it lay empty and deserted by the seashore.

As I gaed doon by Doonsoo Brae,
   Ae bonnie day, ae bonnie day,
I see'd my sweetheart bigging hay,
   Ae bonnie day, ae bonnie day.
The sun, he kissed her bunnet blue,
The wind, he made a richt tae do.
'Eh, lad,' says I, 'I'll dae it too,'
   Ae bonnie day, ae bonnie day.

Anon.

3. Spring and Summer

Spring burst upon the Island with exciting suddenness. I don't remember it as a time of slowly unfolding buds and the hesitant stop-start of spring in other parts of the country. There are no hedgerows and trees to creep timidly into leaf and the country-side never has that unsatisfactory piebald appearance with some trees in full fig whilst others remain stubbornly bare and austere.

As a child spring always started for me on the day when the cattle were let out. All winter they remained chained up in the byre until one magical morning when it was decreed that they could be let out to grass. The field gates were opened and every-thing cleared from their path. Then their neck chains were loosed and whoever opened the byre door flattened himself against the wall so as not to be trampled underfoot in the first hectic stampede. They rushed through the doors as wild as steers at a rodeo. Matronly milk cows tossed their horns and kicked their heels like frolicsome calves in the fresh air and galloped from end to end of the field, their tails curled high over their backs, bellowing with delight that the long winter months were over.

Then we knew that spring had really come. The crops would soon be sprouting and, for the first time, you noticed that the lady's smocks and the primroses were in full bloom.

At first the cows were not allowed to stay long on the rich grass or they would eat themselves to satiety and beyond, but each day their period of freedom was increased until they had settled into the comfortable summer routine when they only came in twice a day to be milked.

Children brought up in the country and particularly on an island like ours have a wonderful heritage which stays with them all their lives. We found the life that went on around us so absorbing that we had little need for toys. Although I believe our parents indulged us with all manner of playthings I have no recollection of them now, whilst the long hours spent out-of-doors remain firmly fixed in my memory.

Springtime meant for us long walks out to the headlands to see the birds as they congregated into colonies for the nesting season, for on the inaccessible cliffs the sea birds came to nest in their thousands. At a distance the cliffs appeared smooth and, in places, overhanging so that there would not seem to be a foothold for any kind of life. As we got closer we could see that the whole cliff face was alive with birds. Predominant were the little kitti-wakes, the smallest of all the gulls, turning and soaring in the draughty air and changing direction by an almost imperceptible alteration in the pitch of their outstretched wings. When caught against the light their feathers took on the translucent look of fine Dresden china.

There was not a crack or cranny of the weather-scarred rocks which was not occupied by the birds. The immaculately-coated guillemots, each with its solitary, sharply-pointed egg, sat in closely-packed rows; everywhere there were the brightly-painted puffins which are called tammy-norries on the Island – which is almost as delightful a name as kirsy-kringlos which is what they call the daddy-longlegs – and on the flat rocks awash at the foot of the cliffs, or standing stiffly upright on the ledges of the cliff face itself, were the dark sentinel cormorants.

In spite of the fact that there were no trees or hedgerows the variety even amongst the inland birds was wide. There were a dozen different types of duck on the lochans which are scattered over the Island and birds which are rare in other parts of Britain, like the hen harrier, are comparatively common. So is the ventriloquist corncrake whose harsh call seems to come from any direction but the correct one. When you do put up a corncrake it would seem that all it can manage is a few yards of ungainly flight before flopping down again yet, when the time comes for it to migrate, it covers great distances over the sea. There were curlew and golden plover and snipe in abundance, none of which was regarded as a game bird by the islanders, with the result that they were left in comparative peace to multiply.

The puffins, which are dull little birds in the winter, acquire a new, wonderfully-coloured outer sheath for their bills in springtime and take on an absurd and festive appearance. They start their nesting operations in April, at first staying ashore only in the daytime and disappearing out to sea at nightfall. Soon, however, great flocks of them are busy with the nesting, burrowing into the sandy soil to lay their eggs or unblocking the tunnels where they had nested the previous year. They become so preoccupied with their tasks and with squabbling amongst themselves that you can sometimes pick them up off the ground. Then they glare at you with a look of outraged dignity, opening their blue, red and yellow striped beaks and turning their heads in search of some way of getting their own back. When you put them down, however, they at once return energetically to whatever they were doing.

During the nesting season all the birds are wonderfully tame. The eider duck will continue to sit on their soft downy nests pretending not to see you when you stand over them. You can even put your hand under them to see if their eggs are hatched while they pay no more attention than broody hens. Only the terns and the plover leave their nests to swoop down on your head, uttering wild cries of alarm.

The chief enemy of the nesting birds is not man but the black-backed gull. If the nest is left unguarded for a moment it will pounce on it and devour impartially the eggs or the chicks in a matter of seconds. The parent birds take turns in guarding their nests and, when the chicks are hatched, fly in turn out to sea to catch sand eels and young herring to feed to them. As they grow into fledgelings, the parents bring back bigger and bigger fish, until the cormorants in particular can be seen stuffing their young with fish so large that it is a wonder they can ram them down their throats.

Perhaps the most remarkable of all the myriad birds to watch are the seagulls. At first sight their nesting colonies appear to be in a constant state of clamorous confusion but watched with closer attention it can be seen that all is order and method.

There are over forty varieties of gull in the world ranging

51

from the tiny kittiwakes to the great black-backs. If a count were taken there would probably prove to be more of them than any other species. It is because of the vastness of the gull population that their community life has to be hedged around with so many strictly-kept rules. Where a pair of nesting golden eagles might hold sway over fifty square miles of territory, a pair of nesting gulls in a gullery are lucky if they can claim five square yards of their very own; but their area *is* their very own and woe betide the intruder who sets foot over the invisible line which marks the boundary.

On the Island the herring gull with its white belly and grey back and black-tipped wings is the commonest. Like all gulls it is monogamous, keeping the same mate for year after year. With the coming of spring herring gulls collect together from all over the islands on their traditional nesting grounds. Each community has its elders already paired off together and its young birds and widows looking round for a mate. The mating ceremony is simple and delightful to watch. It is generally the female which makes the running, circling round her chosen mate and uttering a soft, seductive crooning noise. If the male is attracted he puffs out his feathers and struts to show off his manly charms. If there is another male in the vicinity for him to drive off, so much the better. As a final act of devotion the male will regurgitate some delicacy for his bride and the life-long compact is sealed.

Once the nesting grounds are chosen, the community lives by an intricate set of rules. Trespass is the cardinal sin. If one gull puts a foot out of bounds the owner of the land will lift his wings in warning. If the intruder persists, the other will shoot out his neck or, most dire threat of all, will pull angrily at the grass. If the intruder reciprocates, the fight is on, but usually such a drastic warning serves as a sufficient deterrent.

The rule of no trespass is one of the first the young chick has to learn. To forget it is to be struck dead with a single blow. The second thing that the chick must learn is the way to obtain its dinner. There is a red spot on the underside of each adult gull's beak. Only if the chick pecks at this spot will the parent bird disgorge its meal. So hedged around with convention are the gulls that the parents will let their chicks starve to death if they fail to observe the formalities. This strange ceremony also works in reverse as one lady naturalist discovered when trying to rear an orphaned chick. Nothing would persuade the chick to open its beak until she remembered about the red spot. She put a dot of lipstick on her thumb. The moment she held out her thumb the chick pecked at it and then fell upon its meal with a voracious appetite.

Altogether springtime is festival time on the Island, and the whole pace of living quickens. People start getting up earlier and housewives start turning out their houses and go about visiting neighbours whom they have seen less often through the winter months.

Whenever the subject of living on an island is brought up there is always someone who says, 'I don't think I could stand the loneliness.' It is an odd thing that people should associate islands with loneliness. Perhaps they are thinking of Rockall where only half a dozen men have set foot in the last fifty years or of the evacuated island of St Kilda out in the Atlantic beyond the Hebrides where the roofs of the once snug crofts are falling in and the doors of the farmhouses bang in the wind.

They are lonely places certainly, as the big cities are lonely places with nobody to give you so much as a good morning in the street. There is no more cut-off place in the world than a rented room in a friendless city nor, by contrast, any less exclusive society than an island community. What the city dweller really fears about life in the country is to be cut off from the refuges of the lonely. A world without art galleries and concert halls, without cinemas and without even bus queues and crowded railway stations, is to them a lonely place indeed. But it is not so at all.

To pass a stranger on the road without a greeting is regarded on the Island as the height of bad manners, for there is always time for the ordinary civilities. A stranger is, of course, a rare bird and of immense value for conversational purposes. All the people on the Island know one another and drop into one another's houses when they have some news to impart. It is surprising how much there is to discuss in a closely knit community with communal interests. Births, deaths and marriages are perennially fascinating and there is always some social occasion or another to look forward to or to discuss in retrospect.

Before tractors made their appearance to make ploughing a mechanical operation rather than an artistic achievement, the annual ploughing match was one of the great annual events. One ploughing match in particular sticks in my mind.

Father and Mother took their farming very seriously and Father in particular was always keen to try out new ideas which might prove of benefit to the Island as a whole. The experiments which ended in disaster have for some reason remained in my memory much more clearly than the successes. The most extra-ordinary things used to happen. Once all the baby ducks got into the water tank in the garden and drowned. One hen that we had grew only quills instead of feathers so that it looked like a hedge-hog. There was the broody hen sitting on eggs which, when I peered in inquisitively at it, flew up and pecked me on the end of my nose and fell back stone dead with the exertion. It gave me a great feeling of power. When my parents built the most modern pig house the Island had ever seen, all the baby pigs born there inexplicably died. It was some time before it was discovered that they were being poisoned by some ingredient in the latest type of cement which was being used for the flooring.

It was this misfortune which made the ploughing match such a memorable one. When the piglets died they were buried by my mother's orders in the field next to the house which had lain fallow for some years. The following spring, Father was asked to provide a field for the annual ploughing match and un-wittingly selected the field which had served as the pigs' cemetery.

There was no braver show than used to be put on at these matches. Every piece of harness was polished to the standard of the equipment of the Horse Guards on ceremonial parade. The horses themselves were groomed to perfection, their manes and tails plaited with straw and many-coloured ribbons. As for the ploughmen, they wore their best Sunday suits and their faces glowed from the vigorous application of soap and water, while their ploughs were as freshly painted and shining as the day they had been delivered from the dealer. The furrows that they cut and the turf they turned over were as straight and regular as a ruled margin, so that it took an expert to judge between them.

On this occasion, when the whistle blew, they all started off in fine style, the sun glittering on their panoplies and their ribbons flying bravely in the breeze.

Naturally we boys were all out for our own ploughman, Tommy Rendall, to win, for had we not spent weeks before helping him with the preparations for the great day? It was Tommy who first met with disaster. His plough suddenly gave a jump and there was a great jagged edge to his immaculate fur-row. A moment later and another ploughman suffered the same fate. Soon there were ploughmen cursing in the most ungentle-manly ways as more and more baby pigs were turned up by the ploughshares. The day they ploughed up the Captain's pigs is still vividly remembered on the Island.

Tommy Rendall was one of our great childhood friends. When Father eventually left the Island and moved south Tommy came with us and remained in Father's employ for many years. The most glamorous thing about him in our eyes was that he always claimed that he knew the 'horseman's word'. This was a secret word, known only to a select few, which, when whispered in a horse's ear, had the effect of making the wildest horse do as it was bidden. To our intense mortification, all the years Tommy was with us he would never let us into the secret.

Another of the men who worked on Father's farm, I only remember because of a disaster which befell him. His name was Jock Miller and he had the distinction of as fine a set of side-whiskers and moustaches as you could wish to see. One day when we were playing on the foreshore of St Catherine's Bay we were alarmed to hear in the distance an outbreak of such roars and bellows as to send us at once hurrying in the direction from which they came. There was a small, swampy lochan just back from the seashore and when we topped the bank we saw what had happened. Jock had been ploughing too close to the edge so that his plough had tipped over into the water carrying both Jock and his horse with it. By the time we arrived panting at the scene of the drama only half a horse was to be seen and all that remained in view of Jock was his bald head and luxuriant moustaches. Every time he opened his mouth to let out another bellow he blew a fine spray of mud and water into the air, so that he looked for all the world like an extremely angry bull seal. He was so firmly stuck in the ooze that all we could do was race as fast as our legs would carry us back to the house for help.

Eventually by dint of much heaving on ropes both Jock and his horse were saved from a muddy grave – an operation the success of which was gravely endangered by the hilarity of the rescuers at the sight of the poor man in his undignified predicament.

One of the joys of springtime on the Island was that it brought with it the season for catching spoots. The spoot is the name given on the Island to the razorshell fish whose long, hinged shell is washed ashore empty all around the coast of Britain. With the change of the moon in the spring equinox there comes the phenomenon of the neap tides. Instead of the usual ebb, the sea goes out and out until practically the whole of the sandy bed of the bay is exposed. It is the signal for everyone to grab some sort of a container and a long knife and to rush down on to the newly uncovered sand, for this is the only time when the spoots can be caught.

The spoots live under the surface of the sand and give away their presence by creating a small blow-hole. The technique of catching them is not easy and it requires a lot of practice to become sufficiently quick and dextrous to get enough to make a meal. The most usual method is to walk backwards, bent over to study the sand, with the knife poised ready for action. As you pass over a blow-hole it will probably erupt suddenly which means that the vibration of your step has caused the spoot to take fright and do a crash dive deeper into the sand; its sudden movement causes a jet of liquid to spout up out of the sand, which is how it gets its name. Before it makes good its escape you must plunge your knife into the sand and, with a sharp circular motion, bring the spoot to the surface. A good spoot-catcher will know exactly which way the spoot is going and where to plunge his knife in. He will collect a bucketful in no time at all, while the amateur is lucky if he is successful in one out of ten attempts for, despite their appearance, spoots are fast movers in the wet sand.

It was many years afterwards that I learned that there are better ways of catching a spoot. On the sands at Weymouth small boys arm themselves with a wire hook which they manipulate dextrously to bring the shells to the surface. There is an even easier method. By pouring a little table salt into the spoot's blow-hole it will immediately shoot to the surface of its own accord, prepared to surrender rather than endure the increased salinity of the water. I cannot help feeling, however, that this is a rather unsporting trick.

They are considered a great delicacy on the Island but they require the most expert cooking to make them palatable. Mother's first attempts at spoot cooking when, by our combined efforts we had managed to collect a bucketful, were not a success. Knowing that they were inclined to be tough, she decided to get over the difficulty by the simple expedient of boiling them for hour after hour before serving them up with a white sauce. The more they were boiled, the tougher they became so that the result was a series of short lengths of rubber of a consistency similar to what I imagine might be achieved by cooking leather boot-laces.

The correct method is to drop the shells into scalding water just long enough for them to open and then cook them lightly in milk. Done this way they are supposed to become quite tender and taste, as so many other dishes are described, 'just like chicken'. Personally I have never had spoots which do not taste at best just like the insides of golf balls but I am still prepared for there to be a first time.

All in all there could be nothing more fascinating for a child than the seashore. Each day there were new discoveries to be made amongst the flotsam and jetsam washed up on the sandy beaches as well as the delights of such occupations as making a collection of sea shells or going lobster hunting with a stick. There were few houses on the Island without its collection of shells placed in a bottle on the mantelshelf and we were no exception.

The most prized shells of all were the grotties-buckies, more generally known as cowries which, I have been told, are used by some African tribes as a form of currency. I can well believe it for they are, of all shells, the most wonderful to possess. They are by no means rare but their beautiful smoothness and delicate colouring give a great pride in ownership. Grown-ups, we discovered, were not immune from the excitement of a cowrie hunt. Otherwise boring, female relations could be safely set to the task and would become so absorbed in it that we relied on being left to our own devices without being subject to their constant admonitions. When we had got suitably wet and dirty we could return to find them still busily engaged on hands and knees and with a satisfactory number of shells to add to our collections.

Lobster hunting amongst the rocks was another absorbing pastime. In the spring and early summer the lobsters crawl in from the deep water to hide amongst the rocks while they go through the process of changing their shells. They dig themselves into the soft sand under the rocks between the high- and low-water marks, to hide themselves from the world until they are fit to be seen about again – for a lobster without its shell is a poor and defenceless creature indeed. It is a matter of rummaging amongst the rocks at low tide to see where they have hidden themselves for they push the sand out from under the rocks as a fortification against their enemies. It also gives away their lair as surely as if they had hung out a sign.

Having found your lobster all that is required is a good stout stick. Push this through the sand and wait for him to grasp it in his vice-like claws. Then withdraw the stick smartly and the lobster, unable to disengage himself quickly enough, is yours. If luck is on your side he will not yet have cast his shell and will be at his best for eating. After the old shell has gone, his flesh becomes for a time soft and watery and he should not be given to an enemy.

As spring turns to summer the days grow longer and longer until, by midsummer, the sun scarcely dips below the horizon before it rises again. The crops ripen slowly, the cattle browse on the lush grass and the whole Island seems to drowse in the sun.

Although the Island lies in the far northern latitudes – in fact on almost the same latitude as Cape Farewell in Greenland and the wastelands of Canada – the warm waters of the Gulf Stream keep an equable temperature all the year round and make the land amongst the most fertile in Scotland, matching the rich areas of Midlothian and the wealthy acres of the Vale of Strathmore.

Rich the land is indeed, but it would not be the Island if it did not have some pecularities of its own. Bees and potatoes, both subject to all manner of afflictions in other parts of the world, have never been known to suffer from any sort of disease. Oddly and perversely few potatoes are grown and bees are seldom kept despite the fact that for many months the Island is literally covered with flowers. Gordon and I each had a hive of bees at one time. One night the wind swept mine out to sea never to be seen again, whilst Gordon's, equally insecurely anchored, continued to flourish mightily.

Unfair quirks of Fate like this inexplicably continued to favour him over similar ventures for many years. It was always my possessions which broke first, my animals which died and even my school books which went mysteriously missing.

Once my mother gave us each a tiny Fair Island sheep, which, in the goodness of time, were expected to produce lambs. As it turned out Gordon's gave birth as scheduled whilst mine remained stubbornly barren. When being questioned by a well-meaning but tactless aunt on my animal's biological shortcomings, and desperately trying to present the matter in the best possible light, I am supposed to have announced proudly, 'Well, you see my sheep is a virgin.' I may have put a brave face on the matter but deep down inside me I felt badly let down by the whole business.

Just to be contrary, corn is the name reserved on the Island exclusively for bere, a cereal not unlike barley which is grown nowadays, so far as I know, nowhere else. It is a fast-ripening crop which differs from barley in that the grain grows right round the stem and the beard is immensely prickly and clinging. It used to be a great joke for us as children to put an ear of bere up a stranger's sleeve and ask him to try to shake it down, whereupon the ear works its way quickly and uncomfortably upwards so that he has almost to undress completely to ge it out again whilst we would dissolve in uncontrolled laughter.

Bere meal is used for making home-brewed ale and for milling into the finest flour from which bere-meal bannocks are made. The bannocks, or scones, have a distinctive flavour which is an acquired taste for most people. Spread thickly with home-made butter and sandwiched around Orkney cheese, however, they are held in reverence as a delicacy by the islanders and are sent as a nostalgic treat to exiles all over the world.

When, at the onset of summer, work on the land made fewer demands on the Island farmers' time, they turned their attention to other ways of making a living. There were fishing and lobstering to occupy them and the business of making kelp to be attended to.

Kelp is made by the burning of the tangle, a long, stick-like form of seaweed which grows out on the skerries and which breaks away in the stormy weather and, if the wind is right, gets washed ashore in great profusion.

The burnt ash was used in those days for the manufacture of iodine. It was quite a profitable business and some of Father's tenants used to pay their rent in the form of kelp which he used to send off to a chemical company in England, until some clever scientist discovered a synthetic substitute which killed the industry on the Island and caused quite an upset in the economy.

The long process of kelp-making really started in the dark winter months with the collection of the tangles. It was hard, back-breaking work. Sometimes, after a big storm with a south-easterly gale, the kelper could find enough tangles, delivered as it were to his front door, to keep him carting for days. Equally the sea could, just as easily, sweep it all away from his part of the foreshore – for each kelper had his own territory – and throw it up again on somebody else's.

Most of the kelpers preferred not to leave it to chance. After a stormy night they would be out in the grey dawn, peering to catch a glimpse of the dark shadows in the tumbling breakers which meant that there was loose tangle to be taken ashore. When a man could pay his rent with a few tons of tangle snatched from the ocean, it did not do for him to lie abed.

When it had been dragged above the high-water mark on to the short, springy turf it was piled on low, loose-stone bases to dry out. There it remained, suitably secured, all winter, gradually losing its water content until four wet tons of it had shrunk to one ton dry.

With the coming of the better weather in the early summer the operation of rendering the tangles into kelp by burning commenced. It was a picturesque and highly skilled task. On the first warm days of the year the whole foreshore would be lined with slow-burning fires, the acrid, blue smoke drifting lazily across the Island. All day long the kelpers would tend their fires, piling fresh tangles on the embers from time to time to stop them from bursting into flame and so ruining the quality of the hard-caked residual ash.

The kelping was the cause of endless squabbles amongst the islanders. Territories were jealously guarded, but it was not unknown for a store to disappear mysteriously in the night from one part of the foreshore and appear equally mysteriously on another. Father's services were much in demand as arbiter in these disputes and, whatever the rights and wrongs of them, his word was law.

Another major activity and source of income to the Island at this time of the year was the arrival of the herring boats. Because the Island was blessed with one of the best and most sheltered of harbours in northern waters, it had long provided a base for operations for the fishing-boats from faraway ports. As long ago as the Middle Ages they used to sail north from Holland and Germany for the summer fishing season and sell their catches at the fish auctions on the Island.

After the Great War many of the sailing boats were already being equipped with engines which, by increasing the range of operation and lessening dependence on the weather, made their dependence on the Island harbour less absolute. By a stroke of misfortune, too, one of the first sailing boats to resume operations after that war ran on to a stray mine and was lost with all hands, and this had a very discouraging effect.

Just the same, when we first knew the harbour as children, it was still a thriving place with enough boats putting in each week to justify a dozen or so big fish-curers maintaining their agents on the Island. Over a weekend there might be as many as five hundred boats in harbour and, when the crews gathered ashore on a Saturday night, they had to work in shifts behind the bar at the pub to keep pace with their appetite for beer and whisky. Not unnaturally fights were frequent and it took three policemen all their time to maintain some semblance of order amongst the boat hands letting off steam after their week at sea. I have been told that the single street was as busy as Piccadilly Circus on Boat Race night, and nobody got any sleep until the small hours of Sunday morning.

Whenever a big catch of herring was reported we used to go down to the harbour to see it unloaded. Most of all we used to love to watch the fisher girls as they worked at the gutting. They sat in long rows, chattering at the tops of their voices whilst their hands flew so fast that you could scarcely follow their movement. A herring was grasped and, in a faster time than it takes to tell, it was slit up the middle and the guts cast one way and the clean fish flung with unerring aim the other way into a barrel. The guts were not wasted for they were spread on the land as manure. The effect was to impart a phosphorescence to the oats. If you went out to the barn after dark, the threshed oats heaped on the floor glowed with a blue light in the darkness and, when you ran them through your hand, fell in a gleaming river of light.

The fisher girls were of all ages and a colourful lot. They followed the herring fleets as, with the changing seasons, the shoals of herring moved down the coast. There are fewer of the race nowadays, I imagine, but they still exist, living as hard a life as it is possible to imagine for a woman, although they always seemed to be merry enough about it. It was the fisher girls, not the colonels in their West End clubs, who were the basis of the port trade in this country. Their traditional drink was port and lemon and, if the port they drank was not of rare vintage but Tarragon, it was still a valuable business for the wine merchants. The port shippers in their panelled city offices knew a lot about the movements of the herring shoals in the North Sea by the orders which came in for barrels of their wine from the fishing ports.

Behold congenial Autumn comes,
The Sabbath of the year.

'Ode on a visit to the country in Autumn'
(*John Logan*)

4. Autumn and Winter

The changing seasons of the year are clearly marked for the islanders, not only by the weather and the lengthening and shortening of the days, but by the changes in their way of life which each season brings.

The bringing-in of the harvest marks the end of summer and presages the long winter nights to come. It also heralds the start of the social season, if such a grand description can be applied to a tiny, isolated community.

Of course, the harvest itself is a sociable occasion when farmers are at their most neighbourly. They help one another in turn with the loan of carts and horses and each labours on the other's farm so that by co-operating they get both harvests in sooner.

Our task used to be to help to carry the harvesters' tea out to them in the fields so that the work would be interrupted as little as possible – baskets full of thickly-cut sandwiches, a huge kettle full of black, heavily-sugared tea and a pail of home-brewed ale.

There was a festive flavour about these alfresco meals and everyone went to work with renewed vigour after them. One extreme example of neighbourliness remains in my memory. It was the year Tommy Rendall had had all his teeth out. Teeth are not the islanders' strong point and many of them have their false set before they are scarcely out of their teens. Tommy chewed away at his doorstep-thick sandwich with his gums for some time without making much impression on it. Finally, in exasperation, he leaned over to Jimmy, his neighbour, and said, 'Give us a shottie wi' your teeth a meenit, Jimmy, 'till I get this crust chewed.' Without a word Jimmy took out his shiny new set of gnashers and handed them over. I remember feeling mildly surprised that my mother was so shocked when I casually mentioned the incident to her.

After the harvest was in, everybody had more time to relax. The Harvest Home dance would be arranged, the Women's Institute would resume their social evenings, the Boy Scouts would become active again and the football season would start in earnest.

Despite the dictum in the Old Testament that a house divided against itself shall fall, the Island flourished mightily whilst supporting two factions which divided it neatly in half. For such a small island the difference between the north end, which included the village was mostly rich agricultural land, and the south end, which was more rugged and largely heather-covered, was most marked.

We were south enders and Father encouraged the distinction by constantly issuing challenges to the north end to compete at various sports. For some long forgotten reason we south enders were nicknamed the Pirates and the name has stayed to this day.

Football matches between the Pirates and the rest were contested in an atmosphere of cup-tie fever. Skill may not have been of the highest but great were the deeds of valour on each side when they met. Of course such refinements as football boots had never been heard of. The teams played in their big, tackety farm boots. A few of the younger ones, back from the war, had shorts and a widely contrasting variety of coloured shirts, but the older men simply took off their jackets and galloped into action in their everyday trousers supported by braces. Not a few kept their caps on, for the true islander feels undressed out of doors without his cap, but what they lacked in sartorial elegance, they made up for in enthusiasm. The yells of encouragement from the players to one another as they thundered up and down the pitch often drowned the frenzied cheering of the partisans on the touch-line.

As spectators we had the inestimable advantage of having our war cry to shout. 'Up the Piiii-rates,' we used to yell in unison, whilst the other faction had to content themselves with yelling incoherent advice to their players. Not the least considered supporter of the Pirates was Father's dog, Bet, a formidable-looking but playful golden retriever, whose leash we hung on to with might and main to stop her joining the game. Once Father got the ball somewhere in the middle of the field and was making a determined rush towards the enemy goal. He had only the fullback to beat when, in our excitement, one of us let go the leash. In a flash Bet shot on to the field and seeing the full back advancing purposefully towards her adored master, promptly seized the seat of the unfortunate man's pants and pulled with all her considerable strength in the opposite direction. I can't remember now if this constituted a foul or not but, after the incident, the opposition took to looking fearfully over their shoulders whenever Father had the ball – to the great advantage of our side.

Autumn, too, was the time when Father and Mother used to ask friends up to stay from the south. True, odd aunts and other female relations used to put in an appearance in the summer but they did not make much impression on us. They used to want to take us for tiresome walks or, with a mixture of modesty and great daring, take off their shoes and stockings to paddle in the sea and shriek at the coldness of the water. None of them came up to our exacting standards as epitomised by our beloved Miss Johnstone.

The men who came up for the shooting were a different matter. They were rather awesome, tweed-clad figures but we admired them greatly. There was a General who seemed to us to be incredibly old, although I do not suppose he could have been much over fifty. He was tall and intimidating and extremely absent-minded. Once, when the guns were gathered at the front door of the house ready to move off, the General missed his wrist-watch and I was sent off to his bedroom to find it. I searched with growing panic on his dressing-table for as long as I dared to keep him waiting. In the end I had to go and confess that I could not find it – an admission which caused a great deal of huffing and puffing. When later we took out a picnic lunch for them, I noticed that he had it on his wrist, but I did not dare to say anything.

There was another guest who was even older than the General and who used to shoot with a muzzle-loading gun which greatly intrigued us. The end of the barrel was trumpet-shaped and flames and black smoke belched out of the end of it whenever it was fired. Father said he was the best snipe shot he had ever seen.

5

Our favourite visitor by far was our Uncle Douglas who had emigrated after the Great War from the Island to Canada, where he made and lost a fortune several times. Amongst other ventures he had run a football pool which had prospered mightily until he had got bored with it and sold out. The group who bought it filled in all the winning coupons themselves and finished up in jail.

Uncle Douglas was full of the most exciting stories about the rugged life in the West, for he had once owned a trading station in Alaska which supplied the goldminers and lumberjacks. He also had a vivid imagination which invested the most commonplace with drama and glamour.

The driving mirror in Father's car, for instance, was not put there, as we might have imagined, so that the driver could see the road behind him. It was there so that the driver could see if any of the passengers in the rear seat were planning to stab him in the back. Gordon and I believed his stories for years before the cold light of reason forced us regretfully to abandon them.

As the winter nights get longer and longer, the Island draws more into itself preparing, as it were, to live off its own fat until the spring comes again. This preparation for hibernation is not entirely an atavistic instinct born of the long gone years. In winter, even today, the Island does become more isolated. The inter-island steamers run less frequently and sometimes even the curtailed schedule cannot be kept on account of the storms which can cut off the Island for days on end. New faces are seldom seen and the outside world seems a long way off.

All through the winter the sun only appears fitfully and on some days scarcely seems to rise above the horizon. Then is the time to stay inside around the fire unless you have urgent business to take you out-of-doors, and the islanders, thrown back on their own resources, live their lives in much the same way as their forefathers did.

The plan for winter living was a sensible one. In the old days most of the Island's farmhouses formed part of the same building with the byres and stables so that the family could tend their stock without ever leaving the building. From the outside it presented blank walls to the elements with only the minimum number of embrasures and doors. There was what was known as an oddle hole out of the byre for drainage purposes and a square hole half-way up the wall of the stable through which dung could be thrown out on to the midden.

The living quarters usually consisted of no more than two rooms known as the 'but' and, opening out of it, the 'ben'. The ben served as the sleeping quarters for the farmer and his wife and also did duty as a cellar where the home-brewed ale was stored. All the furniture was improvised from locally available materials. The dresser, or bink, was made from a large slab of smooth blue stone and formed the principal piece of furniture apart from the kitchen table. The master and his wife occupied high, straw-backed chairs which are still known as Orkney chairs and which may occasionally and surprisingly be found in Chelsea's antique furniture shops where they fetch a high price. The children squatted on straw-covered stools made from the bristly stiff grass which grows on the moorland.

The but end of the house was divided in the middle by a fireplace, the portion of the room farthest from the door being known as the in-by and the other half as the out-by. The roofs were of thatch or stone and what light there was filtered in through the sky-lights. There are none of these old houses on the Island today but I can remember visiting one built on this traditional plan and can still recall the pervasive acrid smell of smoke which always seemed to hang about the room and the rivulets of steamy, soot-black condensation which trickled constantly down the walls from the thatch.

Even today a cottager, greeting you at the door of his house, will still say 'Come along in-by', and a small house is still often referred to as 'a but and ben'.

The winter was the time to be busy about the house. To go visiting in the winter was to find the man of the house busy mending his lobster pots or making new ones, whilst his wife would be hard at work at her knitting. Even the children would be engrossed in some task, for they were brought up to be either useful with their hands or their heads.

It always used to be claimed that Scottish children had a better education than the English and, of the Scottish children, the islanders had by far the best scholastic record. I do not think this was anything to do with the rival merits of the educational systems, but due to the long winter nights when a child who was so minded could pore over his books without there being any alternative distractions competing for his attention.

Winter, too, I remember as the time for funerals. Gordon and I were quite expert on the subject of funerals, for the cemetery was up on the hill above our house and to get there the procession had to wind its way past our garden gate. One funeral I remember in particular because of the retribution which followed it. The chief actor in the drama, if one can so name the corpse, was Mr Pottinger, a fat, jolly farmer who was a near neighbour of ours, and of whom we had been very fond.

When the solemn procession came into view we were seated, Gordon and I, one on the top of each of the two stone pillars on either side of our front gate. Instead, however, of remaining in respectful silence as the coffin passed we were both seized with an uncontrollable fit of the giggles. Worse, carried away with hilarity, we started waving to our acquaintances in the procession and shouting quite inappropriate greetings to them. The more ferocious the sidelong glances we received from the outraged mourners, the more we shouted and cheered until we almost fell off our gateposts with merriment. There was no merriment, however, when Father inevitably got to hear of our disgraceful behaviour and we were sent off to apologise contritely to the bereaved family.

The islanders' attitude to death, as in all uncomplicated societies, was a strange mixture of superstitious dread and light-hearted acceptance. There are certainly as many jokes about wakes as there are about any other aspect of Island life.

Winter was also the traditional time for courting and the one was often mixed up with the other. It was the custom that the dead should be laid out in the best room in the house and be watched over until the time came for them to be buried. It was also considered reverent that, no matter what the cause of death, the body should remain in the house for a period of eight days during which time all mirrors in the house had to be kept covered and all cats kept out of doors. In most cases these old superstitions are no longer observed, but the body is still laid out and all relatives and friends are expected to call in to view the deceased and take a glass – whisky for the menfolk and wine for the women.

The long vigil was usually undertaken by three young men and three girls from amongst the family's relations and friends. In this way the long watches of the night were often the occasion for much hand-holding and surreptitious petting to while away the hours, and many a romance was forged during the wakes.

One of the good if somewhat macabre stories of death is still well remembered. It is of an old farmer who was, in the opinion of his wife, long past his time for the cemetery. In spite of repeated hints he remained stubbornly alive until, becoming fed up with her nagging, the old man decided to play a trick on her.

One night, sitting by the fire, he pretended that his last hour was fast approaching. His wife, in accordance with the custom, at once sent out for the neighbours to come in and attend to the 'straiking', as the ceremony of laying-out the body is called. With his friends around him the farmer nodded in his chair until his head finally fell forward on his chest. Even then they were unwilling to touch him, until the wife lost patience and exclaimed, 'Men, hid's high time tae tak' him.'

As they were carrying him through to the ben end he suddenly revived and, seizing a stout stick which he had laid conveniently near, he dealt one of the bearers against whom he held a grudge a severe blow on the head. For fully a minute the whole company stood aghast until the insensible man regained consciousness and, scrambling to his feet, shouted, 'Confound thee, Jamie, thoo's be a hunner an' ninety-nine times dead afore I come to straik thee again!'

The omens and portents of approaching death are to be seen everywhere and in the most everyday occurrences. If a rainbow is seen to touch the ground at two points within the same parish, it is a certain sign that death will occur very soon within its span. The most common warning of all is the 'dead jack', which is the name used to describe the sound made by a woodworm working in a beam. To hear its rhythmical ticking is as sure a warning as it is possible to have.

The crowing of a cock after dark or the sudden howling of dog in the night are generally taken as an omen that death will shortly occur and if you dream that you have lost a tooth you can expect to hear very soon of the passing of a close friend or relative.

On the Island there were always a number of women who had the reputation of 'having a way with the sick', and they were generally regarded as also being the possessors of powers to foresee death and their pronouncements were listened to with respect. One thing is quite certain: when a death had occurred there was no shortage of people to come forward and claim to have heard or seen a portent. In earlier times they would have risked being done to death as witches.

After the chesting – the putting of the body in the coffin – the funeral became an entirely male affair, no women – not even the widow – being allowed in the funeral procession or at the graveside. If the coffin had to be carried for any distance, the oldest man at the funeral walked in front to count the number of steps before the bearers laid down the coffin and the new ones took their place. It was not an envied job as there was a tradition that the man who counted the steps would be the next one to be chested.

Drink customarily played a large part in the proceedings and the straiking was often made the excuse for the frequent passing around of the bottle. When the body was chested, however, the proceedings took on a great solemnity. Once, as the procession was nearing the churchyard, the bottom fell out of the home-made coffin. This sudden disaster struck such terror into the hearts of the mourners that they fled for their lives. It took a great deal of the passing of the bottle before some of the bolder spirits could be persuaded to return to the scene, and turning the coffin upside-down, complete the interment.

There were times during the long winter months when it seemed impossible that the rocky, storm-bound headlands would ever again be carpeted with flowers or that the sun would ride again high in the sky and turn the green, foam-flecked sea into a calm mirror of blue. Even many of the hardy sea birds would have fled from the inhospitable scene, travelling far south on their distant migrations. The kittiwakes would have gone. High in the snow-filled skies the great skeins of geese would be seen passing on their way to the warm south, and the arctic terns would have departed on the strangest of all migrations from the Arctic Circle, across Europe, and down the African coast until some of them would finish up on the even bleaker lands of the Antarctic.

Only in the houses of the islanders the pulse of the Island continued to beat strongly and warmly. Around the hearths the old stories would be told again and the happenings of the year recalled and laughed over. When there were folk in for the evening the fiddle would be taken down from the top of the cupboard and the nights filled with music whilst the sounds of storm beat upon the windows.

What golden days of childhood they were and what a bleak day it was for us when Father announced one winter's night that he was going to sell our fine house in the spring and that we were going to go to school in the south.

Looking back now it seems a great pity, but perhaps living on the Island was never a very practical proposition for our family. The long dark winters did not suit Father's health so well as the more equable climate of Aberdeenshire where we were to settle, and the business of a three-day journey every time we went to school or returned for the holidays would have proved difficult. None the less we were miserable and even the promise of seeing forests of high trees, which we only knew from pictures and which we were promised we could climb, did little to console us.

In fact we looked forward to our first introduction to 'civilisation' with some trepidation. In our childish imaginings trees represented a jungle where tigers stalked. Our remote, bare northern isle seemed a safe and comfortable refuge compared with the unknown terrors of the south where, we were quite convinced, wolves roamed and, for all we knew, savage tribes of cannibals lay in wait.

On our last morning we had been got up at an extraordinarily early hour and dressed in unfamiliarly smart clothes for the great journey. Suddenly, just before we were due to leave to catch the boat, we remembered our rambler rose. Quite where it had come from I cannot now remember but we had planted it with the most loving care against a wall in a sheltered corner of the farmyard and tended it every day. We were determined at all costs that it would survive the rigours of the weather; now we realised that we were leaving it unprotected. Panic-stricken we rushed out of the house and, finding some old sacks, draped them on corrugated iron sheets around it. It was all we could think of on the spur of the moment.

It is funny how things like that stick in your mind. I don't think Gordon or I ever mentioned it to each other again in all the years that followed. But Father died during the last war and Gordon got special leave from the Army to take back his ashes to the Island for burial in the family grave up on the hill. I was stationed in the north of England at the time and, when he wrote me one of his rare letters to tell me about it, he added as a postscript, 'By the way, I looked for our rambler rose but it wasn't there.'

Then I realised that I had had it at the back of my mind for all those years. That it had not survived seemed to me terribly, terribly sad.

Part Two

SONS OF THE ISLES

There is a spell woven by restless seas,
A secret charm that haunts our Island air,
Holding our hearts and following everywhere
The wandering children of the Orcades;
And still, when sleep the prisoned spirit frees,
What dim void wastes, what strange dark seas we dare,
Till where the dear green Isles shine low and fair,
We moor in dreams beside familiar quays.

Sons of the Isles! though ye may roam afar,
Still on your lips the salt sea spray is stinging,
Still in your hearts the winds of youth are singing;
Though in heavens grown familiar to your eyes
The Southern Cross is gleaming, for old skies
Your thoughts are fain and for the Northern Star.

Duncan John Robertson.
(*Quoted in Ernest Marwick's* Anthology
of Orkney Verse.)

5. Return to the Island

My memories of the Island stayed with me vividly in the years that followed but somehow the opportunity of returning never presented itself. By the time school was over there was a war to fight; and after the war there was a living to earn which took me to many parts of the world as remote from the scenes of my childhood as it would be possible to imagine.

Every now and again there would be something to jog the chords of memory – an Orcadian name in the newspapers, the lonely stranger who offered me a drink in a Tangiers bar and turned out to be an islander and another one who was steward on a boat plying between Lisbon and Madeira. Once I was stopped in my tracks in an Oxfordshire village by the faintest whiff of peat smoke hanging in the air. After careful inquiries, I found that I had not been mistaken. A family from the north, visiting their married daughter, had brought down with them a sackful of peats in the boot of their car as the greatest treat they could think of giving her.

And so the years slipped away, one by one.

I was sitting one morning at the desk of my flat in London,

gazing at a blank sheet of paper in my typewriter. It was a particularly cold, wet March day. The wind was blowing gustily around the street corners and the rain spattered intermittently against the windowpanes.

I find nothing more unendurable than winter weather in a city. In the country, if it is not exactly pleasant it can be coped with. In a city where you are constantly required to make hectic sorties from one heated building to another and are at the mercy of the caprices of public transport, everything seems suddenly twice as difficult to achieve and there are few winters when I at any rate do not contract a series of virulent colds.

So it had been this year. Now the book which I was trying to write had become firmly bogged down, so that after each session the floor around my desk was strewn with crumpled balls of paper.

When my wife, Diana, came in from shopping to announce that she had spent half an hour waiting for a bus and that the price of meat had gone up again, I decided that we had had as much as we could stand. I suppose everybody gets these moods from time to time, when the world becomes a grey, unattractive place. Then, if you can, is the time to be up and away. It is one of the compensations of being a writer that, in theory anyway, you can do your work anywhere and the newer the scene the better. There is no train to be caught every morning and no daily routine to tie you to an office desk.

'Let's go up to the Island,' I said to Diana suddenly. In the three years we had been married and I had often talked about the Island, painting it with glowing colours of childhood and promising that one day I would take her up there. It had become a sort of never-never land joke with us for, whenever it looked as if we could take a holiday, something had cropped up which had sent me hurrying off in the opposite direction. Now all Diana said was, 'When?'

'Tomorrow,' I said recklessly. 'Or perhaps the day after.'

In practice, of course, it was not as easy as that. It was not only a matter of cancelling appointments and stopping the milk. The journey had to be planned, arrangements made at the other end and all manner of unconsidered last-minute details to be attended to. Not least of the factors to be reckoned with was our son, Charles, who was just at the stage of taking his first perilous steps and my yellow labrador, Mist, who was getting out of condition and bored with the restrictions of London life. We decided, too, that we would stay on anyway into the beginning of summer on the Island and that we would let the flat while were were away.

What with one thing and another, although we took the decision to go that morning in March, it was not until late in April that we finally dropped the keys of the flat on the house agent's desk and started the long drive up the Great North Road.

In prospect, it is a stimulating experience to put your house on your back and set off into the blue. I had often done it in my bachelor days, but to the married man it does present certain domestic difficulties which do not occur to the escaping prisoner at the moment of decision. Charles was just of an age when he required two Sherpa porters of his own to carry all his equipment. Every spare inch in the car seemed to be taken up with piles of clothes, awkward boxes of toys, a folding pram which did not fold quite enough to fit in easily anywhere, and enough suitcases and anonymous cardboard boxes to make it impossible to see out of the car in any direction except straight ahead. Diana and Charles squeezed up together somehow in the back and Mist curled up on the floor in front under the pile of luggage on the seat. Under these conditions it takes three days of dedicated motoring to reach Scrabster on the north coast of Scotland where you get a boat across to the Mainland.

It was, I suppose, unlikely that the journey would be completed without incident. All went well until the last leg. We had spent the night before with Gordon, now a sheep farmer in a Perthshire glen with an almost grown-up family, and then pushed on over the Grampians. On a remote stretch of road we stopped to allow a learner driver to turn into a side road and she promptly rammed us. She was an extremely pleasant, middle-aged lady who seemed as surprised as we were to find herself in such a predicament miles from anywhere.

There was little harm done so, after we had exchanged names and addresses, we hurried on to our destination for the night. It was not until we arrived, late and tired, at our hotel that we discovered that Mist was no longer with us. Accustomed to her travelling curled up in a tight ball and concealed by the piled luggage, I had not missed her. Now I realised that she must have slipped out of the car at the scene of the accident and had been left in the middle of nowhere a hundred miles behind us.

I remembered all the stories I had heard of dogs making their way back to their homes many hundreds of miles away and enduring untold hardships on the journey. I could visualise Mist loyally making her way back to London to arrive weak from starvation at the door of our empty flat. After endless despairing and ineffective telephone calls I suddenly remembered that an old army friend lived somewhere in the area where the accident had occurred. By a miracle of good fortune and diligence he found her next morning wandering disconsolately near the place where we had left her. She was put on a train and caught up with us in the islands three days later.

Before leaving London I had written to a friend, Erlend Clouston, head of one of the oldest families in Orkney, who lived on the Mainland. We had last met at school when I had been the dignified age of nine and had not corresponded since. Remarking how nice it was to hear from me after a mere matter of thirty-four years he said that of course we must come and stay before going on to our Island. Thus it was another week before we caught the little inter-island steamer which was to take us on to our final destination – a week of typical island hospitality so that Diana's first impression of island life was an enthusiastic and rosy one.

It is one of the considerable pleasures of life to show off a place you know and love well to an audience with no knowledge of it at all. It is, however, a pleasure which is tinged with the anxiety that the audience should see it through your eyes and appreciate it by your standards. Few of us have the delightful arrogance of the flower lover who used to invite his favoured guests into his garden with the words, 'Come and let me show you to my roses.' The onus is usually and illogically on the object to exert itself to live up to your expectations for it in the eye of the beholder.

I was somewhat crushed, therefore, when the first view my family had of the Island was a flat, low, featureless outline, half hidden in a damp mist. Worse, when we started to unload our untidy collection of cases and boxes on to the tiny quay, the fog closed down in earnest so that if Willie Miller had not been there to meet us with his van we would scarcely have found our way the few hundred yards to his house where we were staying.

Fortunately, when we drew the curtains the next morning, the sun was shining brilliantly. One window gave a view over the harbour while the window on the other side of the room looked out over the limitless expanses of the Ocean. I think it was at that moment that Diana stopped worrying for the first time about whether she had turned off the gas in the flat or double-locked the front door.

Of course the first thing I wanted to do was to drive down

78

to the Pirates' end of the Island and show Diana the family house about which she had heard so much. Immediately after breakfast we borrowed Willie's van again and set off, frequently almost running into the ditch as I leaned over first to one side and then to the other, pointing out landmarks and houses I remembered. 'That's where my Aunt Nint used to live! There's the doctor's house!' and so on. Of course it all meant nothing to Diana but it was a great excitement for me.

The journey from the village seemed incredibly short. It was only a matter of minutes before the house came into view, where I remembered it from childhood as a long and exhausting walk. And could this possibly be our great family mansion? We stopped at the garden gate and peered over it at a house shrunk out of all recognition. The shape was the same and it looked much as I remembered it except that it had dwindled to doll's-house proportions. A moment later and Harriet, who lives there now and used to look after us when we were very small, came down the path, 'I ken fine who ye are, come awa' in,' she said, as if it was the most natural thing in the world that I should be leaning over the garden gate thirty-eight years later.

Once inside the house and the memories came rushing back. Even the private smells typical of every well-lived-in house were the same – the smell of wax polish in the hall, the comfortable peaty smell of the little parlour which opened out of the kitchen. Soon we were seated round the fire drinking tea and eating the familiar home-made bannocks and playing the lovely game of 'Do you remember?' Occasionally Harriet would break off in the middle of some reminiscence and look at me and say, 'Oh my, oh my, but you're a big laddie now!' It made me forget my forty-odd years and the grey of my hair.

It was the same wherever we went on the Island. People would come up and shake me by the hand and say, 'Ah, but you've been a long time in coming back.' It induced a wonderful feeling of belonging.

One old man said, 'And is your faither aye keen on the fitba'? He was a great man for the fitba',' then he smiled gently when he realised that Father had been dead these twenty years and that if he was still alive he would have been in his seventies.

It is not surprising that, for the islanders, time should be foreshortened, for each day merges into the next until a week or a month or a year has slipped past. In the cities there are always buildings being torn down and more modern ones being erected in their place so that the scene is constantly changing, marking 'the years that the locust has eaten'. The signs are too frequent and too clamorous to be ignored. There is a race against time in every job and every relationship, spurred on by propaganda and slogans shouted on all sides. 'Time you got a salary increase.' 'Time you got married.' 'You are too old at forty. 'Hurry! Hurry! It's later than you think.'

On the Island we found that the regular pattern of life had an almost mesmeric effect, like driving a car on a long straight road with no milestones to mark your progress.

It is hard in retrospect to say exactly how each day was filled and yet time never lay heavily on our hands. Each morning after breakfast Diana would set out on a shopping expedition and, even if there was nothing in particular that she wanted to buy, this was always a time-consuming operation.

You could, in fact, by stepping outside our front door see the whole of the village at one glance. It consisted of a couple of dozen grey houses standing in single rank along the foreshore. To walk down what, for want of competition, could be called the main street, was to discover that in one of the houses you could buy groceries, in another butcher's meat and that a third was a general store in the fine tradition of general stores. There you could buy anything from shotgun cartridges to fishing lines, from paper doilies to dressmaking pins. None of the shops found it necessary to advertise their wares so that it was only by peering in at the windows that it was possible to discover the emporiums within.

The morning shopping routine was not, however, just a matter of hurrying from one shop to the next. It was the time for the exchange of views with everyone one met so that progress was often held up for half an hour at a time, while the weather was discussed and all the multifarious topics so near to a woman's heart given a thorough airing. Then there was always someone with a cup of tea just ready which would occupy another half-hour, so that an expedition to buy a loaf of bread could well consume the whole morning.

On three days a week there was the excitement of the arrival of the inter-island steamer when almost the whole population of the village would collect at the pier head to see who was coming off the boat and cast a professional eye over the livestock which the farmers were shipping over to the Mainland. For Charles the boat was a never-ending source of wonder and excitement. It no sooner appeared as a small dot on the horizon than he would want to be down on the pier so as not to miss a moment of the business of loading and unloading and be ready as soon as the gangplank was lowered, to clamber up it and renew his acquaintance with the stewards and the deck hands with whom he soon became a great favourite.

The arrival of the boat was, in fact, the only thing which imposed any sort of time-consciousness on the Island. Letters had got to be ready for the mail, for to miss a sailing was perhaps to delay correspondence for three days; the cases of eggs had to be ready packed on the quay for dispatch to Kirkwall; there were people to be met and people to be seen off and even such unconsidered trifles as boxes of library books to be received or dispatched, so that the comings and goings of the steamer always involved a large proportion of the population in one way or another.

As a writer I found the sight of the boxes of books amongst the lobster crates and packages of farm supplies, an encouraging sidelight on the way of life of the islands. It has been said that the two greatest products of the islands are eggs and egg-heads. It is not precisely true but it reflects the pride the islanders take in learning. The standard of education is extraordinarily high and each generation produces its quota of men who make their mark in the arts and sciences. It is unusual if, amongst the portraits displayed proudly in the best room, there is not one of a relation of the house in graduation robes. It is no accident that the county library is the oldest-established in the kingdom and one of the best I have ever come across.

A writer does not have to have more than the most elementary knowledge of arithmetic to realise that the odds against his achieving any kind of security at his craft is on par with the odds against his winning one of the bigger prizes on a football pool. The simple facts are that only a quarter of the population get around to reading even one book a year. Hugh MacLennan, the great Scots-Canadian writer, points out that in America, potentially the greatest book market in the world, only seventeen per cent of all Americans ever buy *one book in the whole of their lifetime.* With the onslaught of television even this figure is showing signs of erosion.

These melancholy thoughts made the lively traffic of books in the northern isles into a small ray of encouragement.

Although the harbour is not the busy place it used to be when the herring fleets used to put in there, there is still plenty going on to keep the inhabitants of the houses which face on to the sea wall, interested. 'There's Archie off to the lobsters,' someone would say, and immediately everyone else in the room would go over to the window to peer through the curtains and confirm the truth of the statement for themselves.

The islanders laugh at their own curiosity. 'You won't get away with a thing here,' said Bunty Miller, in whose house we were staying, soon after our arrival. It was certainly true. An unexpected arrival or departure is known the length of the Island in less time than it takes a rumour to spread down Fleet Street, which is a very short time indeed. One of our neighbours, who spent more than a usual amount of time keeping an eye on what was going on, was known to everybody as the Peninsular. 'She is long and thin and looks constantly out to see,' Bunty explained, enjoying the time-honoured joke.

We had not been on the Island for many days before I myself was the cause of much speculation. It was halfway through the morning when I was busy at my typewriter, and Diana and Charles were on their morning shopping expedition, that I received a visit from the policeman. After a certain amount of humming and hawing and eyeing me gravely, which is the habit of policemen all over the world, he explained to me that he had reason the believe that I was guilty of leaving my car for too long at a parking meter.

In the confusion of our flight from London it was one of the matters I had omitted to attend to and now the inexorable process of the law had caught up with me. There was quite an amount of worried head-scratching between us before we got the matter sorted out satisfactorily, for it was the first time he had had a crime of this sort to deal with and I am a very poor hand when it comes to understanding forms.

With our business completed he relaxed his official attitude and we fell to discussing this and that, so that it was some time before he took his departure.

'You won't be troubled with parking your car here anyway,' he said cheerfully as I saw him off. It was true enough, for the only bit of pavement on the Island runs in front of the house where we were staying and it is used to park cars *on* to keep them out of the way of the cattle being driven to the boat. It is a habit I will have to break myself of, if I ever drive a car in London again.

I had hardly settled down to work again before Diana arrived back, worried and breathless. She had been having one of her endless cups of tea at the other end of the village when someone had come in with the news that the policeman had been to see me, adding, 'and it's something serious because he had his uniform on'.

Everyone had waited with bated breath for him to appear again and when he was a long time in doing so, the certainty grew that it must be a grave matter indeed. Anyhow the policeman's visit had one good outcome. It gave Diana a subject for conversation for several mornings afterwards explaining what parking meters were.

Another arrival at the Island which always excited its fair share of interest was the Bank boat. Once a small pleasure cruiser belonging to a whisky magnate, it now did a weekly round of the northern islands bearing cheque books and money and all the stock in trade of its less mobile brethren.

Sometimes, when the weather was calm, it would come chugging busily round the headland under its own power. At other times it came clipping in under full sail, tacking into the bay with a fine flourish, as trim a sight as you would see in the whole of Cowes week.

Surely no young man setting out on a banking career and with a love of sailing in his bones, could have wished for a finer job than the command of this modern treasure ship.

To do business with this bank was a pleasant if rather unreal experience. Overdrafts did not have nearly the same depressing effect when discussed with a bronzed Viking with a sailing cap on the back of his head and the salt spray drying on his cheeks. Even the money, piled in untidy bundles in a suitcase lying carelessly open, was reduced to a proper unimportance.

I am one of those people who can never pay a visit to the bank or the dentist without a sinking feeling in the pit of my stomach, even if I have not got toothache or have a nice comfortable cheque burning a hole in my pocket until it is paid in. I am always amazed by people who do not suffer from this affliction. One carefree young man of my acquaintance, when writing cheques for horrific amounts in murky nightclubs, has the habit of writing gay notes to his bank manager on the reverse side like 'Wish you were here'. These are heights of irreverence to which only the very rich can aspire, but in my dealings with the Island Bank boat I found I could discuss my weighty affairs with almost equal light-headedness.

We had left our car on the Mainland but, after we had been on the Island for a week or two, we decided to get it over on the

83

steamer so that we would be able to explore the Island at our leisure without the necessity of borrowing a car whenever we wanted to make a trip. To be truthful I had rather left the decision as to whether it was worth going to the expense of bringing the car until I discovered whether Diana liked the Island life. Whilst I had hoped that she would like it well enough to stay into the summer, I was half prepared for the experiment to be a failure, for there was no knowing how someone who had been accustomed to the amenities of living in the south of England would react to such a different way of life.

I need not have worried. Within a short space of time each day was filled with so many important things to do that there was scarcely time to fit them all in. In all our married life I do not think I had ever seen Diana more happy. As for myself I found that I was looking forward to sitting down to a spell of work each day instead of regarding it as the distasteful chore it had become in London.

It was one of the unexpected characteristics of the Island that it gave no sense of remoteness, or rather not the quality of remoteness of the backwoods of Canada or of the vast, still pine forests of Norway. Indeed it invoked a sense of closeness; a feeling of being part of a community which made immediate demands on our loyalty. It was the rest of the world which had suddenly become remote and not the other way round so that, in a very short space of time, it appeared as a far more dangerous adventure to contemplate leaving it than it had done arriving there.

6. Portrait of the Island

Britons are used to being described as an island race and are proud of the description. It is only true, of course, to a degree. Strictly speaking, Australians could describe themselves as islanders and so could practically every other race in the world. The text-book definition of an island as 'a piece of land entirely surrounded by water' can be applied to anything from an atoll to a whole continent.

There are many hundreds of thousands of people in Britain today who have never even seen the sea. I once had a delightful and well-read charlady who lived all her life in Fulham. Until I took her to Piccadilly Circus for a treat on her sixtieth birthday, she had never been farther from her home than South Kensington underground station.

Although his schoolmaster would probably not have agreed, the schoolboy's definition of an island as 'a piece of sea with no water in it' has always appealed to me as a much more apt description. It at least puts first things first, for the great thing about an island is that it should be seen to be an island, with water on all sides. Otherwise you might as well live in Fulham or Bedfordshire or, for that matter, Alice Springs.

On what we had already come to look upon as 'our' Island there was almost no point from which the sea could not be seen on all sides. The land seemed to have pushed itself out of the water like a basking starfish, so that often to reach a point a mile distant across the water meant travelling from the tip of one toe, into the centre of the Island, and then out again. Enclosed by these headlands there were a succession of bays and coves of startlingly white sand which shelved gently out to sea so that you had to wade far out before the water became deep enough for swimming. At other parts of the coastline the cliffs rose sheer out of the water and were indented with deep, mysterious caves which were inaccessible except by boat.

The Island itself rose at no point to more than 150 feet, but the dullness of the landscape was redeemed by the ever-changing mood of the sea and sky, and by the little holms and skerries which lay off the coast and which appeared and disappeared according to the visibility and the state of the tide. Strictly speaking the difference between a holm and a skerry is that a skerry becomes completely submerged at high tide whilst at least part of a holm remains above the high-water mark. It is not always so but it is near enough.

Although there was no car journey which we could make above five miles in distance, the difference between one part of the Island and another was as varied as it is possible to imagine.

During those first spring days the cliffs down at the Pirates' end of the Island were an irresistible attraction, for the myriads of sea birds still invaded the headlands just as I remembered them. Even without going outside our front door the varied bird life around us made itself felt. The desk where I worked stood in a window which overlooked the harbour and from it I could watch the gulls, as the tide went out, searching for shellfish among the uncovered rocks. When they discovered one they would fly with it straight up into the air to crack its shell by dropping it on the rocks below. I was at first fascinated by this show of intelligence. Then I noticed that as often as not they would miss the rocks completely so that their shells landed on the soft sand or even in the sea. I once counted fifteen attempts by one gull before it gave up in disgust. Eventually their stupidity began to irritate me so much that I had to turn my back to the window before I could get on with my work.

To begin with the birds were our main preoccupation and there were few days when we did not make an expedition to some part of the Island to watch them. Before coming to the Island Diana had shown little interest in wild life and used to get considerably teased over her inability to identify even the commonest species. Now she started to enjoy these days out on the cliffs as much as I did and, in spite of the distraction of restraining Charles from plunging to his doom over some rugged precipice, soon became quite an expert.

There were, too, other exciting fields of discovery to vary our days. All over the Island there were the unexcavated remains of earlier civilisations to be found and explored. This profusion of prehistoric remains is common to all the northern isles.

Because of the remoteness of the Orkneys, and of the Shetlands beyond them, they have been saved from the industrialisation which has taken place farther south, so that the material remains of the past have remained undisturbed. The islands have been described as an archaeologist's paradise and it is true. The story of the early history of the Island is all the more fascinating because of the evidence of it which is to be seen on all sides.

Fiften hundred years before the birth of Christ the seafaring races of the Western Mediterranean were finding their way up the coast of France and, crossing the Channel, sailing their frail craft up the west coast of England and Scotland and on across the tidal cauldron of the Pentland Firth to the Orkney Isles, without ever losing sight of land.

They went farther, for from the northern islands of the Orkneys the Fair Isle can be seen on a clear day and from the Fair Isle the bleak outline of Sumburgh Head, the most southerly point of the Shetland archipelago, is visible. Using the Fair Isle as a stepping-stone they sailed amongst the Shetland Isles and, in some cases, settled there. Many more settled in the Orkneys for, in comparison with the Shetlands, they are rich and fertile. In both archipelagos traces of their occupation remain in the megalithic tombs which are typical of the early Mediterranean civilisations, and in the unexplained standing stones which must have fufilled an important role in their lives.

These great sailing feats of the earliest settlers on the islands are impressive but I still like the story of the Fair Isle couple at the turn of the century. They were determined to get married as soon as possible and there being no Minister on the Fair Isle, made the trip to Orkney in a rowing-boat. The ceremony having been performed they then got into their boat and rowed the forty-odd miles back again!

Although, to the old civilisations of the Mediterranean, the Orkneys and Shetlands represented the farthest boundary of the world, the islands have not always been at the blind end of adventure. When the Scandinavians took possession of them just over a thousand years ago the islands became the very centre of their Empire. They stood midway in the traffic between Norway and Ireland and Iceland, providing important harbourages and a place to rest on their warring expeditions. By the ninth century they had colonised both the Shetlands and the Orkneys and, as I have said, the allegiance of the islands was owed to Norway for six hundred years. This is not so surprising when it is realised that the Shetland Islands are nearer to Bergen than they are to Aberdeen.

Of all the vicissitudes through which the islands passed perhaps the most mysterious were the generations during which they were occupied when Rome was the capital of the world. This was the age of the broch builders. The brochs, whose ruined remains are to be found all over the north of Scotland as well as in Orkney and Shetland, were strongly fortified houses whose exact purpose has never yet been satisfactorily explained.

Soon after our return to the Island I took Diana out to see one of their brochs at Lamb Head. It is so well preserved that you can still climb into it through the domed roof and crawl along lengths of narrow flagged passageways, until further progress is blocked by falls of stone. Once when I was shooting rabbits there a terrier followed a rabbit into the broch and got lost in the maze of subterranean passages. It could be heard barking far underground and it was more than an hour before it found its way out again.

The brochs originally were considerable structures, rising as high as fifty feet. Their walls were many feet thick and were constructed on the concave principle revived two thousand years later in the construction of lighthouses. They were either left open at the top or covered with an umbrella-shaped roof made from the ribs of whales and thatched with turf. The doors too were either of stone or whale ribs and hide, working on a stone hinge pivot and fitted with a draw bar so that they could be firmly secured from the inside.

As they date from the time of the Roman occupation of Britain, some hold that they were built as a defence against the raiding expeditions of the Romans. The Norsemen had still to appear on the scene and there would appear to have been no other common enemy from whom such formidable protection was required.

It may have been that marauding bands from the mainland of Scotland put in an appearance from time to time to loot the prosperous islands of the north but the siting of the brochs does not support the theory that they were to repel raiders from the sea. The one at Lamb Head is sited on a rugged promontory where no sea landings would have been practical. Others, as on the shores of Eynhallow Sound on the Mainland, are placed so close together as to be disproportionately thick on the ground from a tactical point of view, while other, more vulnerable, parts of the coast would appear to have been left totally unguarded.

To picnic out on the loneliness of Lamb Head and contemplate what must once have been the populous centre of a half-forgotten race is to be stimulated to all manner of fanciful conjecture.

The immensely thick walls, shuttered entrances and out-defences of ramparts and ditches show that the site was clearly a defensive one but defensive against whom? In the centre of the broch itself there was access to water from a well round which the structure was built so that, with sufficient stored food, the inhabitants could stand siege for a considerable length of time.

So far no archaeologist has visited the Island but sites have been excavated in other islands which have added much to our knowledge.

The evidence of the broch middens on which the refuse of generations of broch dwellers has been thrown, shows them to have lived partly by tilling the land but also to have been seafarers hunting the sea otter and whales. Bones of deer, seal and birds as well as countless limpet shells are to be found in these middens. In the excavated broch at Gurness on the Mainland, the excavators found the skeletons of two human hands still wearing bronze rings, which had been carelessly thrown aside – a grim reminder of some age-old tragedy.

Many of the brochs were extraordinarily elaborate in construction, providing sleeping chambers and communal living-rooms, water-storage tanks, cupboards and open fireplaces. Fixed furnishings like shelves and tables were often made out of stone and survive today as evidence of the way in which the inhabitants lived.

Lamb Head on the Island is only one of the sites favoured by the broch builders. There are many others which are overgrown and long forgotten and no more attention is paid to them by the islanders than to the site of a ruined croft. To Diana and I, however, they were fascinating and to visit a new site was to start off again inquiring and conjecturing. The theory about the broch dweller which I grew to favour was that they were built by the Iron Age equivalent of marauding medieval barons. There is no doubt that they were both piratical and cattle thieves by nature, so that there was little love lost between them and their neighbours and a place where they could defend themselves when attacked was essential. Whether these overlords were an invading race or merely the leading families in the community I would not like to hazard and, in fact, it is not a question which is likely ever to be answered satisfactorily.

What is known is that the need for the brochs had disappeared by the second century A.D. and they had been succeeded by large partitioned houses surrounded by smaller huts to form open, undefended villages and that, such inhabitants as there were, were living peaceably in this way several centuries later when the raiding parties from Scandinavia first put in an appearance.

The Viking Age which starts somewhere around the beginning of the eighth century is one of the strangest phenomena in history and one which had a lasting influence on the islands. The Scandinavian population explosion which then occurred resulted in the Danes, Norwegians and Swedes sending their warlike bands as far as the Caspian Sea to the south and Iceland and Greenland to the west. They robbed and pillaged throughout the length and breadth of Europe, so that their colonising of the Orkneys and Shetlands was only a very small part of a movement which had far-reaching effects throughout the known world.

In the northern isles, however, the effect was probably more lasting than elsewhere for they held on to their possessions there until late in the fifteenth century.

The period of six hundred years during which the islands owed allegiance to the Norse Crown was their golden age. The wild Vikings proved to be good colonisers and, particularly during the second half of their governorship, the islands grew prosperous both as an agricultural community and the centre of northern trade. When the lands passed in pawn to Scotland the picture changed dramatically. Once again they became the end of nowhere and the Scottish overlords exploited the people and deprived them of their rights as freemen which they had held under the Norse régime.

It is little wonder that the islanders look back with nostalgia even to this day to the times of the Vikings, for the Scandinavian culture goes deep below the surface. It took three hundred years of Scottish rule before the old tongue disappeared and many of the words and phrases remain in common use. For example no Orcadian has ever been known to use the word 'little'. The Orkney word is peedie. As they are very fond of the use of the diminutive it is probably the word which strikes the visitor first, for even when the islanders are 'speaking English' words like peedie creep in. After a time on the Island you begin to forget how different the language is. Once, when I was on the inter-island steamer as it was pulling away from the pier in Kirkwall, one of the islanders shouted something to a friend on the quay. 'Excuse me,' said a visitor from the south, 'but what was that language you were speaking?' Incidents like this will delight the islanders, but they will go out of their way to adapt their speech whenever they are speaking to an outsider.

Another relic of the Scandinavian occupation is in the Norse derivation of almost all the place-names in the islands. Most of the islands have the suffix 'ay' from the Norse 'ey' meaning island, and the repeated use of the word 'quoy' in farm names which means an enclosure for cattle or 'geo' meaning an inlet are only two common examples of hundreds of Scandinavian elements. The little holm off the northernmost tip of the Island, where the Norsemen found the Culdee monks in possession, still goes by the name of Papa or Priest's Isle. The Bu farm where the Stevensons live down the south end of the Island gets its name from the nearest Norse equivalent to describe enclosed, manorial land and the two headlands which I would like to think were the first to be sighted by the raiders from the east, still bear their baptismal names of Thor and Odin. It is somehow pleasing that, when they were converted to Christianity a hundred years or so later, the names of their old gods were not expunged.

In the long interval which had elapsed since my childhood I had lost touch with my relations who had remained on the Island, so it came as a considerable and pleasant surprise to find that I still had cousins who lived there. One of them was Mrs Miller, who was a cousin of my father's and whose husband ran the old mill in the middle of the Island in partnership with her son, Jackie Groat.

Indeed it was surprising to find that the mill itself was still going. It was a water mill where the corn was still ground with great round stones and must surely be one of the few remaining in the country. It produced the meal from the bere which was still used to make bere-meal bannocks for which there is still a considerable demand.

One day we went out with Jackie to be shown round the mill by Jimmy Miller, for Jimmy knows every belt and bolt in it. When he gives up I do not know who will be able to dry out the corn and regulate the machinery quite in the way that he does it. It will probably mean the end of another old Island industry.

The first impression we got, that the pulleys and corn lift and the shakers owed something to Heath Robinson, was soon dispelled as we watched Jimmy moving amongst the machinery to give a deft touch here and a shove there, while the grinding stone spun sweetly and the great driving wheel pounded round and round.

It was after viewing the mill that Jackie and I took a walk down the burn which feeds the water wheel and came upon the elvers making their way up from the sea. There were hundreds, there were thousands, there were millions of them. It is impossible to assess numbers when you see elvers on the move, each one a tiny, wafer-thin eel in embryo on the final stage of their dangerous journey across the Atlantic from the mysterious waters of the Sargasso Sea.

The story of the eels is such an astonishing one that it is perhaps worth digressing to tell it.

The life cycle of the eel starts in the Sargasso off the Gulf of Mexico. Somewhere beneath the waters of this sea of floating weeds all the eels of Europe are spawned and from there the larvae start out on their journey. The larvae are tiny and glass-clear. It takes them about three years to grow to six inches and become elvers, whilst they float across the Atlantic on the North Atlantic Drift. Eels of all breeds go through this larva stage. Once a larva was found which was five feet long, which set the zoologists thinking. It is the most convincing proof so far produced that somewhere great sea serpents exist, but that is part of another story which we will come to later.

While the larvae of the European eels drift helplessly across the Atlantic they are beset on all sides by birds and voracious fish, but their numbers are so vast that quadrillions of them survive to swarm up the rivers and, from the rivers, into the tiny streams and ponds until every corner of Europe has its quota, the main body pouring in a flood through the Straits of Gibraltar and on to the Bosporus. This phenomenon takes place every year with millions upon millions arriving at their destination in spite of the depredations on their numbers, so that nobody has been able even to guess at the number which originally set out.

It was some infinitely tiny fraction of these which Jackie Groat and I saw at our feet clogging the burn so that we could have scooped them out by the bucketful. They were on their way to the Muckle Water – the largest loch on the Island but a small loch by ordinary standards.

The elvers stay in their chosen water for six or seven years until they have grown to full size. Then, quite suddenly, two or three thousand eels at a time, they will get the urge to return to the Sargasso Sea to breed. From that moment they stop eating and their yellow bellies turn to silver.

One moonless autumn night they will form themselves into convoys and start off home, wriggling and squirming their way downstream to the open sea. They will not be seen again, for they never return.

Many people regard eels as a great delicacy. Stewed, jellied or baked thousands of tons of them are eaten every year in London alone. They are caught, tragically I cannot help feeling after all the dangers they have survived, at the very moment when their life cycle is about to be completed.

Eel traps are simply constructed affairs, consisting of a narrow gauge grid across the river, blocking the way down but with a convenient hole to one side which leads into a box sunk in the river bank. Once in the box the eels are trapped, for the only exit is through another grid-guarded hole back to the river, whilst the tunnel by which they entered is too steep to be negotiated in reverse.

All the year round the trap will lie empty until the migrations start. Then for several nights the box will be filled to overflowing with homing eels, following an irresistible urge only, at the eleventh hour, to encompass their own destruction.

That afternoon Jackie and I talked about putting in a trap to send our tribute ton of eels to the London market, but we have not done anything about it yet. Perhaps we never shall.

Jackie Groat was, in many ways, a typical islander. Part miller, part farmer, part odd-job man he could turn his hand to anything and was always on the look-out for new ideas. When he came back to the Island after the war, he started a chicken farm which soon became one of the biggest on the Island. Then one night a more than usually strong wind came and blew all his chickens out to sea so he gave up chickens and started in with something else. This philosophical acceptance of acts of God is very much an Island trait.

Jackie is also a source of information on practically every subject under the sun. We were standing one day in his garden when an enormous brown rat splashed into the mill stream beside us.

'We ought to have a rat hunt,' I said, for there is nothing I like better than a good rat hunt.

'There is a much better way than that of killing rats,' he

said. 'You tie a sack needle to the end of a long stick. When you spot a rat, fix it with your eye and walk up to it slowly until you are near enough, then drive the sack needle through its brain. If you never take your eye off the rat it will never move.'

I took this with a pinch of salt but when I repeated the story to somebody else, as one of Jackie's flights of fancy, he said quite seriously, 'Well, of course, everybody knows that is the best way to kill a rat!'

Nobody offered to stage a demonstration, however, so I am still not sure wether I was having my leg pulled, for leg-pulling is one of the favourite sports on the Island.

A typical Island leg-pull is told about an old crofter who lived down the Pirate end of the Island and who followed the usual Island practice of rising with the sun. Some friends returning from a party decided to play a practical joke on him. Taking peats from his peat-stack they carefully blocked up his bedroom window so that, when the sun rose, there would be no light to waken him.

Their victim slept on happily, waking every now and again to discover that it was still dark and going back to sleep. As the day wore on he became more and more restless but, on his wife insisting that she was not going to get his breakfast until the dawn broke, he stayed grumblingly in bed. Finally, just before the sun set, he could stand it no longer. Leaping from his bed he threw open the back door. A moment later he rushed back to the bedroom. 'Get up quick,' he shouted to his wife, 'the end of the world has come and the sun is rising in the west!'

This habit of living by the getting up and going down of the sun has died hard on the Island. When one of the older generation ask the time they will say, 'What time is it by the clock?' as if it were only of interest to know what the clock might have to say in comparison with more reliable methods of telling the time like the position of the sun or the state of the tides.

In fact the passing of time is of so little account that people are seldom in a hurry and punctuality is not considered as much of a virtue. There was one prosperous farmer on the Island whose pride it was to be always ahead of his neighbours with his farm work. His fields were always the first to be ploughed and his hay always the first to be cut. The other farmers regarded this as a most amusing eccentricity. I walked with him up the quay one morning to meet a friend off the boat. There were a number of farmers there collecting their turnip seed for sowing. 'Imagine seeing you, Johnny,' one of them exclaimed. 'I thought you

94

would be busy at the harvest!'

Just the same the Island farmers are amongst the best in the world. In the great agricultural slump in the 1930s many of them moved south to take over farms that had failed and made them prosper, for they believed in the old adage that 'It is the farmer's foot which makes fertile land'. That they also have time to pause at the end of a furrow to watch the sun sparkling on the sea is perhaps their greatest strength.

Like everybody else who lived on the Island, Diana, Charles and I soon fell under the spell of the sea. 'I'll just take a look along the shore,' I found myself saying when there was nothing particular to do. On the shore there was always something worth one's attention: seals playing out in the bay, birds diving for fish or simply the enjoyment of the inexplicable pleasure of gazing out to sea.

So far as Mist was concerned the foreshore was created for her especial delight. She is supposed to be a gun dog with an ancestral tree which has names in it to conjure with in the world of Field Trial Championships. It is a heritage she carries easily – almost, I am tempted to say, with indifference. On the Island my constant efforts to get her to live up to the standard of behaviour I felt I had the right to expect met with little success. On our expeditions along the foreshore I gave up altogether. Although she soon discovered that it was quite profitless to try and creep up on the sandpipers on the rocks, she never gave up trying. The reluctance of the seals lying on the flat rocks at the tide's edge to stop and play with her was also a matter to her of constant surprise and disgust.

The rabbits which lived among the sand dunes were, however, quite a different matter. She dug for them like a mole, completely disappearing down their burrows with only a shower of sand shooting out of the hole to mark the site of her feverish excavations. All too frequently she used to catch one and bring it back to me alive in her mouth, with a look of such self-congratulation as to be quite nauseating. She would then circle round me watchfully to frustrate my efforts to return her prize to freedom. They were usually baby rabbits with the result that the house soon became filled with them. Mist and Charles loved them to distraction and Diana protestingly spent much of her time trying to get them to take milk from a fountain-pen filler. When they were big enough to be surreptitiously released Charles was inconsolable, while Mist set off reproachfully to replenish the stock.

Apart from my constant and unrewarded efforts to control Mist and my preoccupation with trying to keep Charles from falling into the rocky pools, to walk by the sea was a great soporific. I cannot imagine anyone walking angrily along the shore.

The scene was ever-changing; on some days the outline of the neighbouring islands could be clearly seen and, behind them, the high ground of more distant isles piling up against the horizon until they merged into the sky. At other times they were lost in the haze or the soft mist which crept up suddenly to blot out everything to within a few yards.

As the weather got warmer sudden patches of colour appeared magically among the sand and stones. On certain of the stony beaches of the Island the Sea Aster or Oyster Plant grows in great profusion. It is a small miracle how its roots somehow survive from year to year in the shifting shingle to burst out again in a profusion of tiny blue and pink flowers. If you bite the fleshy leaves of the oyster plant you get a distinct flavour of oysters, from which it gets its nickname.

There is a tradition on the Island that it was brought by the storm-harried galleons of the Spanish Armada. I have never seen it in Spain but it is common on the coast of Brittany and on many of our own remote beaches. There is also a tradition that it was the Spaniards who brought with them the secret of the vegetable dyes used by the knitters of the Fair Isle, but I think that both these are pieces of pleasant imagining.

Another rare plant to be found among the northern isles is the *Primula scotica*. Although it is quite an event to come across one, I should say 'comparatively rare' because of a story Robert Rendall, the well-known Orkney shell expert, tells in his delightful book *The Orkney Shore*. On one occasion Rendall visited the great botanist Colonel Johnston. Asked if there was anything in particular he would like to see in the Colonel's collection, the only suitably learned name he could think of on the spur of the moment was *Primula scotica*.

Three hours later, when the time came for him to take his leave, they were still examining variations of the same plant and, as Robert Rendall remarks, 'I had the impression in the end that we had broken off even this limited inspection without reaching any proper conclusion!' Of such stuff are experts made!

□   □   □   □   □

The eels are not the only ones to enjoy the blessings of the Gulf Stream. The Island, as I have already remarked, is in almost the same latitude as the ice-bound tip of Greenland and yet, thanks to the warm waters all the way from Mexico which wash against its shores, it has the same winter temperatures as the Isle of Wight and a much higher one than London. It is indeed a fat, prosperous little island in spite of its diminishing population and as unlike any of the Western Isles of Scotland as it is possible to be.

The Outer Isles of the west of Scotland are pervaded with an air of poverty which, in time, becomes oppressive. I am never quite sure why this should be, for although the soil is poor it can still carry a good stock of sheep, and their waters are as rich if not richer than the northern seas.

It has been said that if the Hebrideans came to Orkney they would soon turn it into another Hebrides whilst, if the roles were reversed, the Orkneyman would soon make the Hebrides as fertile as his homeland. It is certainly not true, but there is truth in it for the main difference lies in the people themselves. The Gaelic people of the Western Isles are a kindly and gentle race but they are at the same time shy and drawn into themselves. They resist change and new ideas fiercely, clinging to the old way of life with an unshakeable stubbornness, as the late Lord Leverhulme found to his cost. Man of vision though he was, with his own fair share of stubbornness, he retired defeated by the islanders' implacable determination not to avail themselves of the millions he was prepared to invest in their future. Even education is regarded with suspicion by the Gaelic-speaking people for fear that their children will see visions beyond the horizon and leave the islands for ever.

The Northern Islanders with their different roots have an altogether different outlook. They grasp at new ideas, hanker after new and better machinery and are hungry for education. The Island is their cradle but the world their kingdom. They are for ever looking outwards, so that they will travel the world and if they like what they see settle where they choose. They are the sons of their Norse colonist forebears and travel is in their blood.

The stranger visiting the Western Isles will not be encouraged to visit the 'black' dwellings where the family share a single room with their livestock, with a hole in the roof to allow the peat smoke to escape. In the Orkneys, so far as I know there is only one such house remaining, which is kept to show visitors and for the islanders to take their children round to wonder at the backwardness of the not so long ago.

In the old days this primitive way of life raised considerable difficulties, not the least of which was when one of the daughters of the house was courting. Her young man would be quite likely to come from another island so that, when he visited her, he would be unable to get back the same night. The rules of hospitality, however, insisted that he should be offered a bed under the family roof. To overcome this difficulty he was put in the same bed as the daughter with a stout centre board fitted between them to satisfy the proprieties. In this state of restricted togetherness the young couple would spend the night, whispering their sweet nothings through an unyielding inch of oak plank.

The mixture of the old and the new is one of the most fascinating features of the Island. In most of what were once stables a gleaming tractor now stands, but many of the crofters still sleep in a box-bed let into the wall and no better substitute has yet been found for the peat stack carefully piled outside each back door. Peat has been the main fuel on the Island for a thousand years and, although Nature is manufacturing very few new peat beds, the supply shows no signs of running out. Peat is made by an ages-slow process from the roots of Sphagnum moss, and is harvested layer by layer from the boggy moorland. Practically every islander has the right to cut peats in some part of the Island, so that coal, which is expensive to import, is little used even to this day.

The name of the Island itself means land of springs and streams and there are still springs bubbling up all over it. Some of them are even below the high-water mark and one in particular was invested with magical properties both by the Culdees and the early Norse settlers. Sufferers travelled from as far away as Denmark to the little Church of Kildinguie for it was said that 'the water of the Well of Kildinguie and the dulse of Geo Odin will cure all things except the Black Death'. The dulse of Geo Odin is seaweed from the caves at Odin Head. It can be cooked to make a supposedly nutritious jelly but the islanders eat it raw. In this form it may be described as edible, but it is my experience that you need to have the teeth of an otter to make any impression on it.

The fame of the Well of Kildinguie is not yet entirely dead for just before my return an elderly sufferer from multiple sclerosis arrived on the Island all the way from Germany to try it curative powers. He stayed for a few days and left loaded down with bottles of water and suitcases full of seaweed.

Alas for the fame of the Island, no word has yet been received of a miraculous cure.

7. An Island Wedding and other Social Matters

'You will be going to the wedding,' said Willie, a few days after our arrival.

'What wedding?' I said. 'Anyhow, we haven't been asked.'

'There wouldn't be many folk going if they waited to be asked. Everybody goes along as a matter of course.'

So, of course, we decided to go as well.

In less remote parts of the country the weeks before a wedding takes place are fraught with the business of compiling lists and of agonised decision-making as to who shall be asked to the Church and who to the reception. The greatest care has to be taken to make sure that no toes are trodden on and that Great-Aunt Agatha gets her invitation in good time, if only to give her the pleasure of refusing it. By the time the original lists have been pruned to the limitations imposed by the size of the bride's house or by the thickness of the bride's father's wallet, there is a danger that the happy couple will start life with as many ready-made enemies as they have friends.

The solution to this problem on the Island was delightful in its simplicity. The whole Island was invited and it was soon clear that, by and large, the whole Island intended to turn up.

Formal invitations were superfluous. The details had hardly been decided upon before the word had gone round and everybody was discussing what they would wear and what a fine couple the bride and bridegroom would make. Just in case some stranger happened in on the boat, there was a card pinned up on the notice board of the general store, alongside the Ministry of Agriculture's notice of new potato regulations and other day-to-day business, to say that Peter and Muriel invited the Island to celebrate their wedding in the village hall at 9 p.m.

By the time the party was due to start the ceremony and the private celebration had been got over with and the wedding party had repaired to the hall to lend a hand getting things ready. When Diana and I arrived it was to find that we were unreasonably early. I should, of course, have known that if the invitation was for 9 p.m. it did not in fact *mean* 9 p.m.

The hall was the scene of frenzied activity. The bride, still in her wedding dress, was in the back regions, supervising an army of helpers in the preparation of mountains of sandwiches and the marshalling of endless cups and saucers. The bridegroom and his friends were hard at work arranging the chairs around the dance floor which, throughout the year, serves in turn as everything from a lecture hall to a badminton court. There was the wedding cake to be cut into slices, later to be handed round amongst the guests with little bags provided for those who might want to send a piece of cake to absent friends, for there are few families on the Island who do not have relatives exiled in some corner of the world. Then there was Slipperine to be scuffled on the floor to the subsequent danger to the limbs of the badminton players and, above all, there was the Bride's Cog to prepare.

The Bride's Cog is undoubtedly the most essential of all the ingredients which go to make up an Island wedding. The Cog itself is about three feet in circumference, made in the shape of an old-fashioned wooden tub except that three of the staves project beyond the rim to form wooden handles by which the vessel can be passed easily and safely from hand to hand. It is girt around by an iron band and the wooden rim is worn thin by generations of drinkers.

The exact mixture which goes into this vast loving-cup varies with each wedding, for each family has its own views on the correct recipe for the Cog. The basis which is common to all is whisky and home-brewed ale, heated to a high temperature and seasoned with pepper and salt and anything else to hand.

On this occasion we watched with trepidation as, in addition to the whisky, a bottle of gin and a bottle of rum were cast into

101

the brew. When it came to tasting it, however, it went down as smoothly as warm milk.

As the other guests began to trickle in, the bridegroom started to circulate round the hall bearing this fabulous mixture, whilst each of the guests in turn drank from it to the health of their hosts. By the time it came to the last ones, the whole vast quantity had been almost consumed so that they had to tip the tub over their ears to reach the final drops of the elixir. Then it was refilled and the whole operation started afresh.

By ten o'clock there was a steady stream of guests arriving by bicycle, by car and on foot. As they shook hands at the door of the hall, the wives and girl friends separated from their menfolk and seated themselves primly on the chairs around the wall to observe the newcomers, exchange gossip and wait for the proceedings to start.

The men at first clustered around the doorway and eventually spilled over on to the floor as the flow of arrivals increased. Even when the band struck up none of them seemed to be anxious to be the first to start the dance. Looking unfamiliarly neat in their Sunday suits and highly-polished shoes, they greeted one another jocularly and shuffled their feet and stole sly glances across the floor at the ranks of waiting partners.

By the time the Bride's Cog had started on its third tour of the room, however, there was a marked effect on the mood of the party. Soon, one by one, they slipped away from their companions to ask the lady of their choice to take the floor, and before long everybody in the room was birling and swinging and stamping their feet. Then, when the music ended, the partners returned to their places like oil separating from water.

As dance followed furious dance handkerchiefs, which had started out carefully arranged in breast pockets, were called into service and jackets were discarded whilst enamel pails filled with beer, alternating with the hard-worked Cog, circulated continuously. Soon the windows were steamed up with condensation and the ladies who had begun by looking so cool in their floral cotton dresses began to get pinker and pinker.

From time to time a break was called. Then stacked chairs were dragged to the centre of the room and the whole company sat itself down to cups of tea and sandwiches and cakes before returning to the reels and schottisches, the lancers and quadrilles, with renewed vigour.

There are no instruments in the world like the fiddle and the 'squeeze-box' to get people dancing; not modern dancing perhaps, but those dances where you do grand chains and figures of eight and whirl your partner round to within an inch of her life. It is thirsty, heart-bursting work which explains another mysterious feature of the proceedings to the uninitiated.

As the evening wore on it was noticeable that, while the number of ladies in the room remained more or less constant, the numbers amongst the men ebbed and flowed to a remarkable extent. An almost imperceptible nod of the head or the flicker of an eyebrow and another group of two or three would slip away until there were only a handful of stalwarts left to keep the dancing going.

Whatever reputation for generosity the host might have, few of the guests would arrive at an entertainment without their private supply of spirits to share amongst their friends. Once outside, half bottles of whisky appeared from hip pockets and were passed round from hand to hand while every topic under the sun was discussed from the price of cattle to the progress of the party.

I found it, at first, a rather unnerving experience, particularly as, not being forewarned, I had committed the great social sin of arriving without my own bottle. It did not make any difference to the amount of hospitality I was offered. Indeed the pace became so fast and furious that for some time I never got back to the dance floor at all before being asked outside again to make another acquaintance and partake of another dram. I never saw anyone produce a bottle in the hall itself but outside, seated in their motor-cars or standing around in dimly discernible groups, there was a constant party in progress so that at times there must have been more people enjoying themselves in the car park than there were in the hall.

The trouble with this clandestine form of drinking was that, taking a swig of neat spirits from the neck of a bottle left me with little idea of how much I was consuming. It must have been considerable, because when I did finally get on the floor I found myself performing the most intricate movements and whirling round and round with the best of them.

It was four o'clock in the morning, when dawn had already broken over the skerries out in the bay, before some of the older folk began to think of making their way homeward. The bride, free at last from her responsibilities of seeing that her guests had had plenty to eat and drink, was making up for lost time, dancing every dance and still looking startlingly fresh in her wedding gown.

By breakfast-time it was all over. 'No stamina,' remarked Magnus Dennison, one of my new-found friends of that evening who had just confessed to me that he was rising seventy. 'Why, when I was a lad, a good wedding used to last for three days.' For weeks afterwards the events of the night were talked about and laughed over. If weddings were not very frequent on the Island, they at least knew how to make the most of them.

Just as the wedding was a free-for-all affair so, we were soon to discover, the social life of the Island was not a formal matter of invitation and acceptance. The telephone had not spread its thin wire tentacles so widely as to be a substitute for dropping in for a chat. To pass near someone's house was to call in and see how they were getting on and, especially on a Saturday night, a chat was more than likely to continue into the small hours of the next morning. Conversation was a leisured business and there was always plenty to talk about where everybody had the same interests as everybody else.

Parties had a habit of springing up spontaneously. If we were feeling sociable, I put half a bottle of whisky in my back pocket and called in anywhere where there was a light burning in the sitting-room window. If we were the first to arrive it would not be long before there were others. The circle round the fire got bigger and bigger as chairs were brought in to accommodate new arrivals. At some stage there was sure to be singing and, as the bottles of whisky passed from hand to hand, the party would overflow to the kitchen to dance. Nobody was in a hurry to go to bed for, with everyone on the Island more or less their own master, what it was inconvenient to do on the morrow could always be put off until the next day. If one Saturday night party showed signs of flagging there would certainly be another party somewhere else which was just warming up. Energy was inexhaustible and time of no account whatever.

It was a week or two before Diana and I got used to this easy-going sociability. Being used to the more carefully regulated social system prevalent in London, where it was unusual to be on better than a nodding acquaintance with your next-door neighbour, it seemed at first an unforgivable intrusion to walk in at somebody's front door without first ringing up, but it was a reserve which we soon overcame.

We were to discover, too, that it was a system which worked equally in reverse. Because our windows fronted on to the main street we were particularly vulnerable and we rapidly found that it was not a profitable occupation to go to bed early to read. At any hour the door might burst open and our tiny sitting-room be filled with a ready-made party bearing their own liquid refreshments. Then there was nothing for it but to get dressed again and join in the perambulations from house to house.

The following morning at seven o'clock, which was the hour at which Charles liked to start his day, we would have had far too few hours' sleep and resolve to have thicker curtains fitted over our bedroom window.

8. The Strange Case Against the Grey Seal

If there is one commodity which is universally popular amongst the islands it is controversy. If there is no common cause on which all the islands can unite to criticise, such as the sins of the Government in power or the ever-increasing freight rates to Aberdeen, they will occupy themselves in proposing the merits of their own island against those of the others. Each island has its own prides and prejudices and each regards the others with a mixture of suspicion and affection.

The inhabitants of most of the islands bear generic nicknames which are shouted proudly by their supporters at a football match or used by the inhabitants of other islands as a mildly derisive description. The people of the island of Westray are known as Auks, a name which derives from the dubious distinction that it was at Mull Head in Westray that the last known Great Auk was shot. The men of Sanday are known as Gruelie-belkies which means porridge-bellies and which they get from their custom of finishing up a night of heavy drinking by mixing a hot toddy of whisky and oatmeal. Likewise, for reasons long since forgotten, Rousay men are known as Mares, Shapinsay men as Sheep and the men from Stromness, rather unflatteringly, as Puddings.

Thus, when the boats are putting back to the islands after a day out in Kirkwall and a group of Rousay men run into a group of Shapinsay men, the night is enlivened by an outbreak of baa-ing and neighing which must sound quaint, to say the least of it, to the uninitiated.

The inhabitants of our Island are known to all other islanders as Limpets. This is supposed to derive from the days when each of the islands contributed a labour force to the Mainland for the purpose of building St Magnus Cathedral, and where they were distinguished from the rest by their custom of living almost exclusively on a diet of these rather unpleasant shellfish.

As I have said, every now and again a subject crops up which rises above inter-island politics and becomes common ground for criticism by them all. One which has become a hardy annual and in which we soon became involved was the controversy which breaks out each year about the culling of the Grey Seal. The correspondence columns of the local paper, *The Orcadian*, are filled with letters of furious denunciation and equally violent defence which is echoed in the national Press, and in homes all over the Island the issue is argued to and fro.

As is often the case when the cause is one which arouses the emotions, much of the argument is hopelessly out of perspective. Wildly inaccurate statements are accepted at their face value and the whole issue becomes clouded in a welter of sentiment.

It is, however, a matter of great importance in the northern isles and, indeed, in a much wider field, so I will attempt to set out the facts around the strange case of *Halichoerus Gryphus* over whose sleek head so much argument rages.

The Grey Seal is amongst the rarest seals in the world. Of all the seal family only the Atlantic Walrus and the Ribbon Seal are rarer by perhaps ten thousand head. At the last count there were about 50,000 Grey Seals in the world. There is a small colony in the Baltic and another in Canada but they are insignificant in numbers. Ninety per cent of the world population of Grey Seals live around the rocky coasts of Great Britain and, of these, by far the largest breeding colonies are in the Orkney Isles.

By comparison with the total number of Grey Seals there are about 300,000 Common Seals in the world and this number is dwarfed by the 3,500,000 Crabeaters, the 4,000,000 Ringed Seals and almost 6,000,000 Harp Seals. These figures put the responsibility squarely on our shoulders to ensure that the Grey Seal survives.

Only fifty years ago the Grey Seal came perilously close to extinction. One estimate, although probably a wildly pessimistic one, put their numbers at a mere 500. It was then that the Government stepped in and introduced legislation to protect them from the rapacity of the sealers – for the fur of the Grey

Seal, and particularly of their newly-born pups, fetches a high price in the European fur market.

The protective measures had the desired effect and the number of Grey Seals rose rapidly above the danger point. Incidentally it was one of the first occasions when a government had brought in effective legislation to protect our indigenous wild life, and I believe the measure was introduced as a direct result of the intervention of King George V. It is sad to think that similarly enlightened measures in earlier years might have saved for us such animals as the Sea Otter, which had the unenviable distinction in the nineteenth century of having the most valuable skin in the world.

To see the Grey Seals today packed in their thousands on their breeding grounds makes it hard to believe in their recent extreme rarity and their continued comparative rarity by world population standards.

There is a tiny holm, not more than ten acres in extent, which lies in the bay just by our old house on the Island. When I first remember it, the farmer who owned it used to put his horses out to graze there in the summer, which was the occasion of an amusing incident. One summer the grazing on the Island had been exceptionally poor and the farmer was being constantly troubled by hungry stock breaking into his cornfield and doing considerable damage to his crop.

My father was his neighbour and it was against him that the farmer's wrath was directed. Father hotly denied the charge but relations remained decidedly cool until the real culprits were detected. Keeping watch one night the farmer discovered that it was his own horses which, finding themselves short of grass on the holm, were swimming over in the dark for a good feed and withdrawing discreetly back to their sea-girt island before sun-up!

This tiny holm where there used to be no seals, is now completely covered with them during the breeding season and has become scheduled as one of the places where a cull can be carried out. Thus, with the annual killing of the Grey Seal pups taking place almost on their own doorstep, feelings were running high on the Island. Nor was this in any way lessened when it was learned, soon after our arrival, that one of the professional sealers who had arrived on the Mainland from England, was intending to make his permanent home on the Island.

It is necessary at this stage in understanding the problem of the Grey Seals to understand something about their breeding habits. In these they are completely different from their cousins the smaller Common Seal. The Common Seal breeds earlier in the year. It comes ashore on the rocky promontories to breed but, almost as soon as the pup is born, it takes to the sea again. Within hours of its birth the baby Common Seal has learned to suckle in the water, clinging tightly to its mother so that even the breaking waves cannot dislodge it.

With the Grey Seal the breeding season is a much more elaborate affair. Several weeks before the pups are born they haul out on their breeding grounds, sometimes travelling quite considerable distances from the water's edge. There have been cases of the mother seals being found as much as a mile inland. As in the well-ordered breeding colonies of many other animals each breeding cow has her own inviolate territory. When the pups are born the mothers stay with their offspring constantly, to suckle them. Indeed, the pup itself is completely immobile and quite unable to gain the safety of the sea if attacked. With constant feeding their skins soon become stretched as tightly as a drum so that they lie on their breeding grounds like so many trussed-up mummies.

The moment the young seal is ready to take to the sea, however, the mother completely loses interest in it and it is left to fend for itself. For several weeks it lives on its puppy fat whilst it slowly learns the art of catching its own food and becoming independent. During this period the whole colony is living in the waters round the breeding ground.

Where the colony is a big one this presents a serious problem to the young seals fighting to establish themselves. With so many of their kind in search of food in the same area, fish rapidly become extremely scarce, with the result that only the strongest and most vigorous of the pups survive. In stating this definitely I would like to add that it is only my opinion but it would certainly account for the great number of emaciated runt seals which are found washed ashore, for example on the Northumberland coast opposite the Farne Islands. It is a phenomenon which has only been observed since the colony has grown so greatly in numbers.

It is while the young pups are in their inactive state that the culling takes place and it is this which has caused much of the outcry amongst animal lovers throughout the country. Indeed the picture of the helpless and enchanting-looking pups being done to death at the outset of their existence is not an attractive one. If it is only anticipating the infinitely more cruel selectivity of Nature, by which many starve to death, it does not appear in such a grisly light.

There is, however, a much more extraordinary aspect of the decision of the Government to lift the ban on the killing of the Grey Seal pups on their breeding grounds, and it is one which has influenced many of the more thoughtful critics into believing that the raising of the ban was unnecessary.

In January every year the salmon reappear from their mysterious sojourn in the deep waters of the ocean to start their journey up to the headwaters of the rivers where they will breed. At the mouth of most of the large salmon rivers there are stake nets which reap a rich annual harvest by trapping the migrating fish. With the increase in the number of Grey Seal the fishery tycoons noticed that they were appearing with increasing frequency in the area of the nets. Often the trapped salmon were found to have been eaten and sometimes the Grey Seals were found caught in the mesh of the nets leaving no doubt as to the culprits. Worse still, their efforts to escape would frequently be successful, with the result that there would be great, gaping holes in the nets through which not only the seals but the precious salmon could escape.

This was a state of affairs which, not unnaturally, infuriated the fishery men and raised considerable indignation amongst the rich and powerful men who owned the bank fishing rights farther up the rivers. They found themselves, in fact, in exactly the same situation as a farmer whose crops are suffering from a plague of crows or whose pastures are becoming overrun with rabbits, and of course, they had the same remedies. The Grey Seal was, however, unfortunate in picking an implacable enemy who had the influence to do something more about it. Questions were raised in Parliament and the Scottish Department of Agriculture and Fisheries was instructed to conduct an inquiry.

The result was a report which was only remarkable in my opinion for the bias it showed against the Grey Seal. That, so far as the Department was concerned, was that. Permission was at once given for the thinning-out of the Grey Seal colonies on their breeding grounds as the only way the Government could think of to help the salmon fishermen who appeared to be quite incapable of finding their own solution.

The case against the Grey Seal seemed to be a strong one, but there was another side to the question as the public were quick to appreciate.

In spite of the depredations of the seals the profits from the salmon nets had not diminished. In fact quite the contrary. Even on that finest of all salmon rivers, the Tweed, which lies very close to the big seal colony on the Farne Islands, the profits had gone up while the size of the colony increased. This, it was argued by the seal protectionists, showed that the Grey Seal took a greater toll of the salmon's enemies like the lump fish than the tribute they exacted from the salmon.

In the Department of Agriculture and Fisheries report there was a case quoted, to support their indictment of the Grey Seal, of a fishery at the mouth of one of the salmon rivers in Sutherlandshire. There, they claimed, the depredations of the seals had become so great that the fishery had to close down altogether. That the seals were entirely responsible was proved by the fact that, when new owners took over the rights, they instituted a vigorous policy of shooting the seals at the river mouth. At once the fishery started to improve until, within a few years, it was as prosperous as ever it had been.

The citing of this case was, in many people's opinion, an argument against attacking the seals on their breeding grounds. If such excellent results could be obtained by vigorous action by the salmon netters in this instance, why could not the other fisheries take similar action in their own interests? As for the torn nets it was easily shown that it was only necessary to introduce stronger nylon nets to minimise the damage.

So far as opinion in the northern isles was concerned the problems of the fishery tycoons were too remote and too academic to make much appeal. The slaughter of the seals on their own doorstep made a much more immediate impact on their emotions and it did appear that the salmon fishers had run crying to the Government for help in a problem which they should have been quite capable of solving for themselves.

At this stage the national Press started to take an interest in the matter and, as is their custom, they squeezed the pips of emotion until they squeaked. There had to be a villain in the piece and this was soon found in a team of young men who had thrown up their careers for the more adventurous life of earning a living as professional sealers.

They were operating in the area of the Wash and soon the *Daily Mirror* in particular was on their tails. Discovering from one of the fur companies that an absolutely perfect seal skin -- which is a great rarity -- could fetch as much as £25 they published a slashing article, pointing to the vast profits which were being made from the hideous slaughter. The suspicion of cruelty

111

to animals has an appeal which never fails to rouse the British public and brings out the best in them. A not so attractive characteristic is the anger which many people feel at the thought that somebody is making good money which they are missing.

The article had an unfortunate side effect to the rousing of popular indignation on behalf of the seals. The following weekend the Norfolk coast was like a battleground with the roar of assorted artillery as people rushed to take advantage of the opportunity of making a quick fortune. The shooting of a seal is, however, a difficult and highly skilled business. Unless it is shot in exactly the right place and at exactly the right moment in the water it will sink to the bottom and be extremely difficult to recover. Most that are shot at by the amateur will be merely wounded and make their escape before they die. That weekend exacted a considerable toll amongst the seals, martyred to the needs of sensational journalism.

The sealers had devoted their attentions in the south to hunting the Common Seal, the shooting of which has never been banned, but which are much more difficult game than the Grey Seal pups whose destruction offers no difficulty. Contrary to popular belief, too, the skin of the Common Seal in good condition is much more valuable.

When it became known that the sealers had arrived in the Orkneys and had applied for a licence to shoot the Grey Seal pups indignation knew no bounds. Added to the fact that they had already been publicly pilloried in the Press was the Orcadians' well-known dislike of outside interference. If seals were going to be shot for a profit, it was at least a profit which was to be earned by the islanders themselves.

The Orcadians have a term for people who come up from the south which is used with varying degrees of affection. They are called 'Ferry-Loupers' which means anyone who has 'louped' or jumped on the ferry across the Pentland. You have to have lived on the islands for a generation or two before you can escape from the description. It is used to poke friendly fun but, in the case of the sealers, they were 'Ferry-Loupers' of the worst description and there were no more unpopular men on the islands.

It is fair to say that the conditions under which the Grey Seal pups could be taken were subject, officially at least, to severe restrictions. They could only be taken from certain overcrowded breeding grounds, licences would only be granted to *bona fide* sealers and the total number they were allowed to cull was limited to seven hundred.

112

The controls were rigidly enforced on the Farne Islands, where the seal could only be killed under supervision; but in the Orkney Isles the administration of the scheme was so mishandled as to reduce it to farce. Licences were granted more or less to anyone who applied for them and their operations were completely uncontrolled. When it was felt that the total number had been reached the licensees were informed by letter of the fact. When the letters were received it was the signal for a final onslaught, for of course nobody could tell that the seals had not been killed the day before the letter arrived! In this way, even the Government acknowledged, the permitted numbers were greatly exceeded. On some of their breeding grounds like the island of Pharay Holm, they were wiped out altogether.

It is easy to see when all these circumstances are put together why there is so much indignation voiced in the island on the subject of the Grey Seals. I certainly think that the lifting of the ban was done for the wrong reasons and that the administration of the scheme so far as the islands were concerned was disgraceful.

On the other hand I am altogether convinced that the 'farming' of the Grey Seal pups on their breeding grounds is a bad thing. From the sentimental point of view it seems no worse than the breeding of young calves to produce veal and with a great deal more point to it than the long dehydrating journey endured without water by the turtles in order to provide an anaemic soup which traditionally graces the banquets of civic dignitaries.

By the time we had arrived on the Island, the culling of the seals had been carried out for several seasons and altogether the indignation broke out afresh each year there was no doubt that the business had become much better regulated. Licences were now only granted to responsible people who owned the holms on which the seals bred or to their appointees. It was in their interests, therefore, to see that the annual cull was conducted in such a way as would preserve the colonies at optimum production, and it may be that the number of pups which starve to death after they take to the water is being greatly reduced.

Just the same, feeling still ran high in certain quarters on the Island when it was known that one of the 'Ferry-Loupers' had actually bought a house on the main street. There were others on the other hand who felt that it brought a much-needed new business to the Island, and there were even reports that the man who was coming was not really such a bad chap after all.

He arrived one morning, swishing into the harbour in his

speedboat with a great flourish, with Diana and I peering furtively out of our window like everybody else to see what manner of a man this was whom we were to have living in our midst.

I met him soon afterwards in the pub and was pleasantly surprised, after all I had heard, to find that he did not have a long tail and horns growing out of his head. In fact I was to come to know Tom Young extremely well in the months that followed. I spent many evenings round at his house and had long discussions with him on the rights and wrongs of the sealing business. He was a science graduate from Glasgow University who had given up the academic life as too tame a way of earning a living. He had all manner of ideas for using modern methods to make his fortune from the sea which was his real love. Conversation with Tom Young was apt to be a rather disjointed affair for, particularly as the evening wore on, he was prone to breaking off what he was saying to launch into one of the old sailing songs and, once he had started on them, there was no stopping him. In this he had much in common with the islanders who are never at a loss for a song and it was not long before he became part and parcel of the social life on the Island.

Tom's argument was that sealing had always been a legitimate occupation all over the world; which is true enough although, until permission was given to cull the Grey Seals, it had more or less died out amongst the islands. Indeed it is doubtful if, at the time of lifting the ban, there were any *bona fide* sealers in the Orkneys to whom licences could properly be granted.

Apart from at the time of the cull, it was his view that an effective sealing operation could only be carried out by a team equipped with a fast boat to ensure the recovery of the bodies and armed with high-powered rifles fitted with telescopic sights to ensure a clean kill. The present system which permits anyone with a small boat and a 12-bore shotgun to maraud at will is simply not good enough. I agree with him.

Apart from the salmoners' arguments (which he agreed with me in discounting) there are good reasons why the population of both the Grey and the Common Seal should be controlled. They do consume vast quantities of white fish and they are definitely responsible for the spread of worm in cod. The seal acts as host to the cod worm and although worm does not preclude the sale of the cod it does have the effect of lowering its quality. Indeed so prevalent is worm in cod from our home

114

waters that, if they were precluded from the market, they would rapidly become one of the rarest of fish and we should be even more dependent on the already considerable quantities brought in from faraway fishing grounds like Greenland.

As the law stands at the moment there is no ban on the killing of seals outside the breeding period and it is in this direction that I believe the reformers should employ their zeal. It is difficult to establish just how many adult seals are destroyed in a year but I believe the number to be considerable. What is certain is that the methods used are far from expert and the equipment used inadequate for the purpose, with the result that many are never recovered. Even the seals that do find their way on to the market are often of inferior quality and fetch correspondingly low prices.

There would seem to me to be an argument for the banning of the shooting of either the Grey Seal or the Common Seal *at any time of the year* by unauthorised persons. The criterion of whether licences should or should not be granted should depend on the ability of the applicant to show that he has both the proper equipment and the requisite skill to carry out the job.

In suggesting the restriction of the sealing operation to a few qualified licensees I am not suggesting that the authorities should thereafter be exempt from the responsibility of imposing a rigorous control on the sealers' activities. As matters stand at the moment there is no doubt that the seal industry is capable of being developed along scientific lines to the undoubted benefit of the economy of the islands, but the numbers taken each year must be clearly laid down on the advice of the most expert opinion available.

Being something of a sentimentalist myself I have sympathy with the sentimentalists in their loud denunciation of the newly-revived seal trade even if their attacks are not always as logical as one would like them to be. Many of them believe that some sort of seal control is necessary, but rise in indignation at the fact that it is tainted with commercialism.

The commercial aspect seems to me to be a recommendation rather than the subject for criticism. By comparison with a properly conducted sealing operation, whaling is a much more cruel affair and the extinction of the whale a much more real problem. The most modern method of killing a whale is to fire a shell which explodes inside the body, from which death results a considerable time afterwards. The death of a seal is, or should be, instantaneous. Nor was there any outcry from nature lovers when

115

shark fishing developed as an industry on the west coast of Scotland, for the shark is as incapable of arousing our protective instincts as the rat or the scorpion.

The seal is as much a commercial asset as the fish which surround our shores or the deer which roam our hills. Looked at in this light I see no reason why they should not play a part in our economy, subject always to the strictures I have mentioned, and I believe I have scientific backing for saying that careful 'farming' can even be shown to be beneficial to the future of the seal population.

The whole question of the preservation of the natural wild life in Britain is a complex one. Every year there are species of animals and birds which are becoming rarer and rarer. Whilst the disappearing animals in, for example, the African jungle excite world-wide concern, the same process is going on outside our own front doors and little notice is paid. The house martin, for example, is a fast-disappearing species in many places, and so I believe is the swallow. The predatory hawks against whom every gamekeeper's hand was once turned, are now in need of rigorous protection. The partridge is another bird much less common in the English scene and it is many years since I have heard the call of the corncrake outside the Orkney Isles.

Strange things are also happening to our indigenous animal population. Some species like the wild cat and the pine marten are actually on the increase in the remoter parts of Scotland, but some of the small rodents like the fieldmouse have become extinct in many areas.

The islands still provide a refuge for some types of birds driven from their haunts farther south and, in fact, the farther south one goes the more problematic the preservation of certain species becomes. The reason is not far to seek. The use of chemical sprays, however much the manufacturers may protest to the contrary, has a grave effect in upsetting the balance of Nature, and the constantly increasing demands for living space made by man is denuding our countryside of much of its wild life. In England, only in very few places like the Lake District and Dorset and the New Forest is there any real sanctuary left.

There is little enough we can do about it, but at least an effort should be made to preserve what territory we have from the selfishness of man. There is, for example, a current agitation amongst the pony breeders in the New Forest to drain certain areas because they find they are losing their commercially valuable ponies in them. I have little sympathy with them. Any New

116

Forest pony worth its salt should be able to avoid such natural pitfalls, as they have done since time immemorial. Indeed it is far easier for the pony owners to keep their ponies safe in the hundred square miles available to them than it is to assess the damage which might result to the rest of the wild life in the Forest if these few isolated marshes are done away with.

All over the country there are men and women who dedicate much of their spare time in fighting to preserve our national heritage, but too often their voices go unheard. The needs of man and his works are too urgent and the juggernaut rolls irresistibly on.

In the battle over the Grey Seal popular opinion and the efforts of unofficial bodies like the Orkney Field Club did much to bring about the better state of affairs which now exists. I have no doubt that when autumn comes round again, the controversy will break out afresh. That it should is healthy and necessary. If a policy on the lines I have suggested becomes effective, which I believe it will, their vigilance will be more than ever necessary. Would that there were an equally lively conscience in other parts of the country.

9. Journey to Sule Skerry

One evening, about a month after we had come to the Island, Diana and I had called in at the pub to have a drink and a chat with the landlord, John Dennison, after a trip to see if the birds had started nesting out on Borough Head.

'The place you want to go to see the birds nesting is Sule Skerry,' said John. 'The puffins will be nesting there in their thousands.'

I knew all about Sule Skerry from hearsay but I had never met anyone who had been there. It was not surprising, for it is officially the most remote of the inhabited British Isles. It lies out in the Atlantic about thirty miles off the most westerly point of the Orkney Isles and about sixty miles from our Island.

The only time it is visited is when the *Pole Star* – the flagship of the Northern Lighthouse Commissioners – goes out once a month to relieve the lighthouse keepers and land supplies. Because of the wild seas which surround the rock, even this service is an irregular one. Often the conditions make it impossible to land for weeks on end and the *Pole Star* only stays the shortest possible time off the island. Even if an outsider could get permission to make the trip on her, there would be no time to explore the island or take more than a cursory glance at the birds which nest there in their tens of thousands in the early summer.

We talked about these difficulties for some time without coming to any conclusion until I said jokingly:

'Well, John, we'll just have to make the trip in your boat.'

'We'll just do that,' said John. It was a minute or two before I realised that he meant it.

John Dennison is altogether a surprising man. I do not know whether to describe him as an innkeeper, a lobster fisherman, a sheep farmer or a lighthouse keeper, for he is all of them in turn.

His day starts at six in the morning when with his schoolboy son, Magnus, he sets out to haul his lobster pots so as to be back in time for Magnus to go to school. A few years ago he bought a sizeable holm off the southeast end of the Island where he is custodian of the automatic lighthouse and where he runs a flock of sheep. During the lambing and the sheep shearing it means his taking a trip out there most days and, in the middle of the day and in the evenings, there is his bar to run; so that it is seldom he gets to bed before midnight. Just the same, if there is someone who wants taking in a boat from one island to another, it is usually John who does the job and, just for good measure, he is the deputy coxwain of the lifeboat.

In his spare time he is an enthusiast for everything from photography to playing the pipes, so it was perhaps not surprising that the proposed trip to Sule Skerry should capture his imagination. Soon we had the charts out on the bar counter and were deep in discussion about tides and weather. It would be an eight-hour journey each way and it was important that we should hit the tides exactly right. The roosts around the island are so fierce that, if they were running against us, the boat would scarcely be able to make headway. The weather too was a vital factor, for it is only under certain conditions that a landing can be made; and, anyhow, I for one did not much fancy being caught in the open Atlantic in a half gale in a small boat.

Just to complicate the issue still further we had a friend who was coming up from London to stay. Roy Dickens is a photographer who travels the world with his camera on behalf of celebrated magazines. He is for ever departing for or returning from some glamorous assignment in the far corners of the earth.

I felt that a visit to Sule Skerry would at least have the merit of introducing him to one of the few places which it was unlikely he had already been to!

As we mulled over these weighty matters, Diana muttered something about getting supper ready and disappeared.

Ten minutes later she was back again.

'That's all arranged. Bunty is going to look after Charles so that I can come as well,' she announced. 'After all,' she added by way of argument, 'you will be gone for twenty-four hours so somebody will have to do the cooking for you.'

Having our own cook aboard was a luxury we had not bargained for, but there is not much profit in arguing with Diana when her mind is made up. And so it was agreed.

For ten days we listened anxiously to the shipping forecasts and rang up the weather station on the Mainland to get reports on what conditions were like at the rock. From my experience in London I knew that Roy was one of those people who always find it difficult to keep a luncheon appointment on the right day, so I was reconciled to not knowing what day he was going to arrive. It was just a matter of expecting him when he turned up.

The wind continued to blow in the wrong direction until, one Friday morning, we got news that conditions were improving. As the lambing season was well under way and the following week John would have to be busy with them every day, we decided it was now or never. The decision to leave that night was hardly taken before the telephone rang and it was Roy announcing his arrival at Kirkwall.

The inter-island boat was not due to sail until the following morning but fortunately Tom Young was going to Kirkwall in his speedboat and he could bring Roy back with him.

He arrived festooned with cameras and drenched with spray and a few hours later we slipped out of harbour on the midnight tide and we were on our way. It had been a lovely starlit night but we had scarcely cleared the harbour before the fog came down, blotting out the beacon lights as we twisted our way through the islands.

Then, when we hit the open sea, the wind started to rise and soon the waves were crashing on the deck in the darkness. In our travels Diana and I have always boasted to each other what marvellous sailors we were; with an inclination to think, on my side, that I was the better sailor of the two. Still, I believe that if anyone had suggested putting back at that moment I would have meekly agreed.

We were all packed in the deck-house but, as the wind increased in strength, first Roy and then I felt that the world might become a bit more stable below decks. To my secret irritation Diana actually seemed to be enjoying the experience and even busied herself making mugs of tea in the windy swaying galley.

The less said about the rest of the journey the better. Every now and again, lying in my bunk, the boat would fall away from under me, leaving me suspended in mid-air. A moment later it would rise again to meet my descending body with a jolt that I felt must be covering me from head to foot in bruises. An occasional muffled groan from the next bunk assured me that the distinguished photographer was not faring very much better. In the end I must have dozed off, for when I was next conscious it was broad daylight and Magnus was shouting down the hatch that we had sighted land.

When I crawled on deck it was to find that it was true enough. When the boat climbed out of the trough of the waves I could just make out the rock through the spray, lying dead ahead. There had been a lot of joking about our missing the rock altogether and finishing up well on our way to America. From the look of satisfaction on John's face, I suspected that he was as relieved as I was! We had sent a wireless message to the lighthouse keepers arranging for them to fly a flag if a landing was possible. Now, through field glasses, we could see that the flagstaff was ominously bare. As we drew nearer we could see the spray dashing against the tiny landing stage cut out of the jagged rocks which surround the island and once more I wrote off the whole project.

We were not to be allowed, however, to give up the affair so easily. When we chugged round to the leeward side of the rock we saw the three lighthouse men standing in earnest conference at the top of an awesome-looking cliff. Most sinister of all they were armed with coils of rope which they were trying in various positions down the rock-face.

The swell was too great for our boat to stand in close to the shore but we had a tiny cockle-shell of a dinghy lashed on the after-deck which, Magnus had told me with some pride, he had made in the woodwork class at school. It was not an item of information which did anything to add to my confidence. If anyone had told me that I was going to have to spring from a wildly bobbing dinghy to grab a flapping rope on the sheer,

121

slippery cliff face and haul my sixteen stone up fifty feet of rock I would have been inclined to pooh-pooh the whole idea. A glance at Roy confirmed that the same thoughts were passing through his head. In fact it was precisely what was expected of us.

John was already in the dinghy dancing perilously alongside, and the moment of truth had arrived. It was at this stage that Diana, who was giving every appearance of having the time of her life, took a hand at settling our indecision. She appeared from below bearing plates on which a glutinous mess was rapidly congealing in the cold air. She had hardly had time to say 'scrambled eggs' before Roy, choosing the better of two fates, was over the side and being rowed rapidly ashore. When later I too found myself, much to my surprise, at the top of the cliff, it was to be greeted by broad grins from Bob Wood, the principal keeper, and his two assistants, Walter Gammach and Ewan Stewart. The least I felt they ought to have done was cheer.

Once ashore, however, we soon forgot the perils we had so recklessly overcome. As we walked up the cement path which led to the lighthouse, the puffins rose in dense clouds all around us. I have never seen birds in such numbers. Every stone was covered with them and, when we reached the lighthouse buildings, they were perched along the roof-tops like flocks of starlings.

Tammy-norrie, sea-parrot, pope, coulterneb or bottle-nose, the puffin by any other name is surely one of the most extraordinary of our British birds. Most of the year puffins live in the wastelands of the ocean. It is only with the coming of spring that they acquire the disproportionately large, multi-coloured beaks which give them such an irresistibly comical appearance, and come ashore for the business of laying and hatching their single egg. Around the beginning of April, they start collecting together in the daytime in the sea off their intended nesting grounds and at nightfall disappear out to sea again.

They seem to remain undetermined in this way for about ten days; then, one morning, they start rising in great flocks to circle round their chosen ground, until first one flock and then another plummets down out of the sky. Immediately they land they start feuding and fighting for nesting space, digging new holes or opening last year's burrows. Each night they return again to the sea and it is not until the laying season is almost due that they start to spend their whole time on land. I had, of course, seen them in the Island but in nothing approaching the numbers there were on Sule Skerry. The sandy soil in the middle of the island was so honeycombed with them that, if we stepped

122

off the path, we sank at once up to the knees through the shallow roofs of their burrows.

With their strutting, self-important ways they are fascinating to watch. They completely possess the island so that it is some time before you realise that there are other birds, too, which have their nesting colonies there, but driven by the very numbers of the puffins to nesting in strictly segregated areas. On the almost vertical sides of one inlet the kittiwakes pack together, miraculously contriving to find a precarious foothold where they can lay their eggs. On another area of barren rock the fulmars huddle together, and yet another bleak cliff-side is black with nesting cormorants. They are hardly to be noticed, however, in the kaleidoscope of colour provided by the puffins.

Even the puffins themselves have insufficient room for all their numbers so that some unlucky ones are forced to lay on the loose shingle on the north side of the island, where they are an easy prey for the predatory black-backs.

When the puffin chick first appears it is a ball of downy fluff like a tiny powder-puff, yet it soon requires the combined efforts of both parents to keep it supplied with food. Within a fortnight the white breast feathers start to appear and two weeks later they are ready to take to the water.

After the middle of July, scarcely perceptible at first, the numbers start to decrease and, by the end of August, they have all disappeared again into the lonely wastes of the Atlantic. The other birds soon follow them, so that by the time autumn comes the whole fantastic circus has gone and Sule is left to keep its lonely winter vigil with only the seals and a few black-backs for company.

I had never been inside a manned lighthouse before and I was almost as keen to examine it as I was to see the birds. Out on the gallery which surrounds the light we could look down on the panorama of the tiny island and the sea around it. Through the haze to westward we could see the 140-foot-high Stack Skerry showing startlingly white. The impregnable Stack is in some ways even more extraordinary than its neighbour. It is the home of the solan geese who inhabit the waters around the rock for ten months in the year. In the nesting season they are so thick upon the cliff face that it takes on the appearance of being an absolutely white pillar. Yet, oddly enough, no solan has ever been known to nest on Sule Skerry or even to fly over it.

In the old days the Hebrideans in particular used to sail to Stack Skerry each year to harvest the young solans which they

123

prized as a food. Landing there is, however, an exceptionally perilous business, and after several lives had been lost the practice gradually ceased. It is probable that nobody has attempted to land there now for over thirty years.

In the top gallery of the lighthouse there is an imposing visitors' book which records all the visitors to the rock since the first foundations were laid in 1895. The intervening seventy years have only sufficed to fill a couple of dozen pages recording the comings and goings of lighthouse officials and the names of survivors from wrecks on the skerry. As the landing conditions had been so bad, Diana had decided to stay aboard. It was, just the same, a pity that she could not have added her name to Roy's and mine, for she would certainly have established a precedent for her sex. As it was we felt that we could safely claim that Roy had established an all-comers record – from Piccadilly Circus to Sule Skerry in twenty-three hours!

About the only thing I knew about lighthouses was that the family business of the family which produced Robert Louis Stevenson was lighthouse building, and that they had built most of the lighthouses which surround our shores. Robert Louis himself was trained in the business and worked at it for some time, but he hated it. In fact, his brave spirit which overcame his own infirmities with such fortitude shrank before the terrors of wind and storm which might be described as the stock-in-trade of the lighthouse builder.

'... the horrible howl of the wind round the corner; the audible haunting of an incarnate anger about the house; the evil spirit that was abroad; and, above all, the shuddering silent pauses when the storm's heart stands dreadfully still for a moment. O how I hate the storm at night! I always heard it as a horseman riding past with his cloak about his head, and somehow always carried away, and riding past again, and being baffled yet once more, ad infinitum, all night long.'*

Drinking mugs of tea with the lighthouse men in their tiny circular sitting-room, I learned much that I did not know before. For example, that in the early days lighthouses were not built out of public money as I had always supposed. They were erected with privately-subscribed funds and paid a good return on the money invested by the levying of a farthing per ton on shipping which passed their way. I asked Bob Wood, who is a veteran in the lighthouse service, if he did not find the two-months-on-one-

* R.L.S. to Mrs Sitwell. *Letters*, Vol I., p. 182.

month-off routine which they do on Sule Skerry a trifle mono-
tonous. 'What really gets me,' he said, 'is the amount of work there
is at home to catch up with during the month off. Just imagine
a garden where nobody has done a hand's turn for two months
and just think of all the odd jobs there are to do about the house!'
I suppose that is one way of looking at it.

In fact, Sule Skerry, in spite of its remoteness, is not regarded
as by any means the worst of the manned stations. Most dreaded
are the lighthouses like Bell Rock, which has no surrounding
land whatever and where the only exercise to be got is climbing
up and down the spiral staircase. Because of the conditions, a tour
of duty on the Bell is limited to six weeks. Even then, when the
lighthousemen come off their walking muscles have become so
wasted with disuse that, when they come to walk on a level surface again, they are subject to violent attacks of cramp.

On Sule they at least have the coming and going of the birds
to watch and a few acres to wander over, if only to get away
from each other. Nowadays the television set provides a distraction from the endless games of draughts and the limited
number of two- and three-handed card games. Even so it is
important not to let the little idiosyncrasies of your companions
get on your nerves, like one of the principal keepers who used to
find his companions so unendurable that during the whole of
his tour of duty he would not address a single word to them. If
he wanted to give any instructions he would communicate
them by note!

As we talked the wireless receiving and sending set, which
is manned round the clock, was crackling with weather reports,
conversations between ships at sea and gossip and personal messages being passed between one lighthouse and another. I had
never realised before that these messages could be picked up on
an ordinary wireless set. When Bob had finished putting over
his routine report he announced, 'Would anyone who is in touch
with Mrs Dennison tell her that her husband and party have
made a safe landing and she can expect them home again on
schedule.' Sure enough someone on the Island was listening and
she duly got the message.

When the time came for us to start the homeward journey we
made our way back to the cliff-top to find that in the meantime
the tide had dropped, so that the view of the return journey down
the cliff looked even more intimidating than it had in reverse.
Courteously I allowed Roy to try it first. Standing on the top of
the cliff while he was being rowed out to the boat, I looked back

125

at the lighthouse. Around the top of the light the puffins were perched in their dozens. As I watched, one after another pushed itself off to go tobogganing down the sloping dome on its stubby tail and launched itself, wings flapping wildly, into space. Then they would wheel around and resettle on the top ready for another slide. It added a delightful Walt Disney touch to the whole proceedings.

Eight stormy hours later and we arrived safely back on the Island. Already the whole adventure had taken on an air of distant unreality, so that it was hard to believe in the tiny rock out in the Atlantic where the little miracle of the puffins was being acted out as it had been since time unremembered.

10. A Living from the Sea

What with one thing and another the question of our returning to London stayed in the background. We had already been on the Island three months and it was August before I broached the matter.

My conscience was pricking me in a vague and unsatisfactory way. When we were living in London the days had never seemed long enough to fit in all the pressing business matters which seemed to require attention. Now I felt uneasy because I could not believe that all the feverish activity of London life could be suddenly halted. Surely, I thought, there must be something I am neglecting. One of these days, I felt sure, the bubble would burst and we should have to go scurrying back to mend the broken fences.

When I mentioned my thoughts to Diana, she looked at me in surprise.

'Don't you realise that you are doing twice as much work as you were doing in London? Why, you even answer letters now and all that sort of thing!'

It was, in fact, quite true.

Every writer has a different way of working. Some find the best time for writing is in the evenings; others like the mornings. Some work in short, sharp bursts; others write for more prolonged periods with less intense concentration. Some can only work shut away in splendid isolation; others like the wireless blaring and the chores of the house going on around them.

I used to find that unless I sat down firmly after breakfast each day for a three-hour session I got no work done at all and everything had to take second place to this daily ritual. On the Island it had worked out quite differently. Each morning at breakfast we would look at the weather and make our plans. Sitting on the beach gazing into space was rated as just as legitimate an occupation as going fishing or taking a picnic out to the headlands or paying a social call down the other end of the Island. Yet I always found time to do my three hours during some part of the day or during the evening, without fear of interruption. Disgraceful though it may sound we planned the day by putting our pleasures first and fitting in the work somehow afterwards. In fact it proved an ideal arrangement and, as Diana pointed out, in some strange way, I was getting far more work done than when I was sticking to a disciplined routine. Even more extraordinary was the attention I found I was paying to my correspondence. During my travels or living in London, I found I never wrote letters. I would spend hours on the telephone or in keeping appointments which I now realised could have been dealt with, with much more economy of time, by letter.

On the Island there were only three outgoing mails and three in-mails in a week. Thus getting the mail ready for the boat became one of the few routine tasks. If one got out of step as it were, it might taken ten days to achieve an exchange of letters but if you hit it right it could be achieved in about half that time. Under these conditions my business affairs, incredibly, began to assume some sort of order. Business friends knowing my slapdash ways were amazed to find their letters being replied to, so that when we did finally come to leave the Island my affairs were in much better shape than they had ever been before.

The Island had imposed a discipline of its own – a rhythm which took its time from the wind and the tides, from the sunny days and the stormy days, and in which the insistent ringing of the telephone and the demands of the appointment book had no place.

The ease with which we had assumed our way of life on the

Island was, I am sure, little to do with us. It is a quality which all islands have. Ulysses discovered it and Gauguin, once he had eaten the lotus, was trapped for ever by Tahiti. Even Robert Louis Stevenson with all his deeply ingrained love of his Motherland could not grant himself his wish to die on his native heath:

Be it granted to me to behold you again in dying,
Hills of home! and hear again the call;
Hear about the graves of the martyrs the peewees crying,
And hear no more at all.

He drifted to his death on Samoa, dreaming the sentimental dreams of home which are the hair shirt which every exiled Scot wears next to his skin and are at the same time his greatest strength. There is no race in the world more easily moved to tears by thoughts of home than the Scots, eating their hearts out on the far frontiers of the world, nor any people less willing to return home if the opportunity offers.

The malady of living on an island is quite a different matter. You get that by contagion and the only cure is to mark a date on the calendar and on that date pack your bags and go.

Summer was the slack season on the Island. Work on the farms was at a standstill while they waited for the crops to ripen. The professional fishermen spent most of their time ashore, repairing their lobster pots and making their boats ready for the stormy weather fishing which was to come. Although summer is holiday-time it is only for the schoolchildren that the word has any real meaning. None of the farmers or fishermen think of seeking a change of scene and leaving the Island to battle with the uncertainties of holiday hotels and the doubtful attractions of crowded resorts farther south. Many of the Islanders have never crossed the Pentland Firth and when they hear the wireless reports of miles of traffic-jammed roads, shake their heads in wonder.

'Man, but they must be a *hardy* lot down there,' one old man remarked to me as he sat outside his cottage reading a week-old paper showing pictures of the Bank Holiday crowds packing the beaches on the South Coast. It is a feeling that certainly most of the older folk share.

Although the fleets of herring-boats have gone, there are still half a dozen seine netters which are locally owned and of course any number of smaller boats, for a high proportion of the Islanders have some sort of craft of their own. From our sitting-

9

room window where I worked and which overlooked the harbour I could watch their coming and going. It proved a pleasant distraction from toiling at the typewriter.

In fact I found it more of a temptation than a distraction. I soon got to know most of the boat owners and when I saw them getting ready to go out on a fine morning I had to be very strong-minded not to join them. Even the little outboards going out hand-lining always seemed to have room for one extra and I knew that to turn up on the pier was to be invited to come along.

One way or another there was always something Diana and I wanted to do and if Charles was not absorbed in some occupation of his own he would tag along happily behind. I suppose in a busier or more objective society most of our ploys would have been described as time-wasting, but it did not seem like that to us.

One of the most impressive of the local boats belonged to Bill Stout. He used her for most of the year as a deep-water lobster boat but she was also equipped for seine netting, and in the wheel-house there were instruments which flashed off and on and a wireless set which crackled impressively with weather reports. Nobody pays much attention to them, for Bill knows the waters round the Island like his own back garden and can tell what the weather is going to be like long before the meteorological stations give their warnings.

With only the small population of the Island as a market, seine netting is not a very commercial proposition. Sometimes they would shoot the net purely to get bait for the lobster pots, for the needs of the Island for white fish could be very easily supplied with one haul a week.

I had never seen seine netting done so when one morning Bill sent word down that he was going out for the purpose, I dropped what I was doing with the utmost alacrity and hurried down to the harbour.

Bill Stout, coxswain of the lifeboat, certainly looks the part. Sturdily built and weather-beaten with the faraway look in his eyes common to men who earn their living from the sea, it would be hard to mistake his calling.

There is a fascination in watching an expert fishing crew at work. On the way out to the fishing grounds Bill leans against the wall of the deck-house with a cigarette in the corner of his mouth discussing every topic under the sun except, possibly, fishing. Occasionally, and without any obvious purpose, he swings the wheel a point or two one way or another whilst the rest of the crew are relaxing on the piles of nets on the stern or somewhere in the mysterious bowels of the boat.

Suddenly, at some presumably recognisable point in the featureless sea, he breaks off a discussion about the techniques of water ski-ing, of which he is a pioneer in the northern isles, to cut the engine to half-speed while the marker buoy is thrown out and the neatly-stowed rope starts slipping out, coil by coil, over the stern. The boat describes a slow circle while the net is cast. Each man carries out his job almost automatically and each movement is timed to the second without, apparently, a word passing between them.

It always seems to me a small miracle how the boat is brought about in a complete and exactly-sized circle back to the marker, with scarcely a glance over his shoulder by the helmsman. Even in foggy weather the tall marker-flag looms out of the mist at exactly the spot where he obviously expected to find it. I once asked Bill how he did it but he just looked at me curiously as if he suspected I was pulling his leg.

With the rope picked up from the buoy, the net is now spread out astern in a bag and the slow trawl begins, the boat chugging at dead slow ahead and rolling with the waves as the winch draws the bag tighter and tighter.

Bill and his crew watch phlegmatically but you can detect just the faintest flicker of excitement as the bobbing corks which mark the net draw close into the boat. As the tail of the net comes to the surface the gulls appear out of an empty sky and dive upon it to carry off such small fish as they can drag through the mesh. Then, as the net is hoisted aboard and loosened, the whole deck is covered in a slippery deluge of wildly-flapping haddock and skate, gurnets and flounders.

For a time organised chaos reigns while the net is slipped again and the catch is sorted into boxes. By the time the next haul has come aboard the fish are all neatly stowed away on the foredeck – and not only stowed away but cleaned as well, with the guts thrown to the swarms of raucous gulls carpeting the water around the boat.

Surely the strangest of the fish dredged up from the depths are the skate, with their almost human lips on the underside of their flat heads, which open and shut in voiceless protest at their treatment whilst their lidded eyes flicker in sad resignation to their fate. The elegant fulmars stand aloof from the squabbling gulls waiting for the skate livers to be thrown overboard to them as they paddle patiently alongside, for the livers are the only part they will condescend to eat. Then even the lordly black-backed gulls hold back, for in spite of their smaller size the fulmars are ferocious in the defence of what they consider their rights.

The most unwelcome catch for the seine netters are the dog fish. There are vast quantities of them in the seas around the Island and the net is sometimes filled with them. Then there is nothing to do but throw them back again, for they have no commercial value whatever. On the other hand the Norwegian boats cross the North Sea specifically in search of dog fish, which they process and export. Just recently a factory to process dog fish has been started in the Shetland Islands but it is too far for the Orkney boats. Perhaps one day someone will think of doing the same on the Island. It would certainly be of immense benefit to the seine netters.

One of the things that strikes a landlubber like me when out on a fishing-boat is the extreme orderliness which prevails throughout the operation. I have always had a sneaking feeling that man is basically far more domestically minded that woman. He cunningly hides his aptitude for household tasks for fear he should not be taken in his own home for the helpless creature he likes to appear. Here on Bill Stout's boat was the proof of it. In all the complicated manoeuvres there was not a coil of rope out of place. After each haul the decks were swabbed down and there was even hot water to wash in after handling the fish. In all the times I was to go out in her, I never saw his boat other than as tidy as the front parlour of a houseproud housewife.

Incidentally the washing of the decks is a sign of the passing of the old days. The older skippers hold a superstitious belief that to wash the decks is to wash out the luck and nothing will induce them to do it until their boat is safely back in port. Fishermen all over the world are, of course, a superstitious lot. The number of things which must not be done or must not be said, are legion. To whistle aboard is taboo and to stick a knife into the mast a cardinal sin, sure to bring bad luck. For the same reason many fishing-boats will not carry a woman aboard or a minister of religion.

To take a boat out to sea against the course of the sun is so sure to bring bad luck that the islanders avoid it as instinctively as a motorist changes gear. For a gull to land on the rigging is a good-luck omen but even to mention some land animals by their correct name is a sure way of bringing disaster. A cow must be referred to obliquely as 'the one that has horns', or a horse as 'the one that pulls the plough', so that the landsman on a fishing-boat must tread warily lest by a slip of the tongue he is responsible for a poor catch.

During the summer one of our favourite evening occupations was to go out in a small boat to hand-line for fish close in to the shore.

Hand-lining is one of the least demanding of occupations in terms of skill but it can be immensely exciting just the same. Diana, who had never caught a fish of any sort before she came to the Island, broke her record the first time she dropped her line overboard. When she pulled a small codling aboard one would have thought, from her cries of delight and astonishment, that she had broken the British all-comers record.

The easiest fish to catch by this method are the kuithes, which is the name given on the Island to the coal fish when it is a year old and weighing between a half and three-quarters of a pound. The same fish is known as a sillock before it reaches its first year and as a saithe after its second year. Freshly caught they are delicious eating.

When fished from a boat only a heavily weighted line is used, with half a dozen or more hooks to which the merest wisp of a feather is tied to act as a lure. The lures are dropped overboard and the line let out until the weight hits the bottom. Then it is merely a matter of raising and lowering the line a foot or two until an excited tugging from below indicates that fish have obligingly attached themselves to the hooks and are waiting to be hauled up.

Sometimes their demands are continuous and as fast as the line is let down again there are three or four more waiting to be pulled up. If you run into a shoal of mackerel the game becomes even more fast and furious, for mackerel, when they are taking, have suicidal tendencies second to none. It is unusual not to find every hook occupied when the line is pulled in, until the bottom of the boat is piled high with them. Mackerel are to my mind the most beautiful of all the sea fish, their streamlined bodies iridescent with purples, blues, greens and silvers which change as you watch them. They remind me in this way, of tiny dolphin, except for their cold fish eyes which put me, quite illogically, out of sympathy with them.

Dolphins, which are occasionally seen in the Island waters, are the gayest of creatures. They seem to delight in human company, showing off wildly as they somersault and dive around the boat and appearing to look at you out of the corner of their merry eyes to see if you are taking it all in.

Once when I was fishing for tunny and swordfish off the Madeira coast I was unlucky enough to hook a dolphin, and the memory of the experience still fills me with horror. To the Portuguese boatman it was a great triumph. He nearly fell overboard offering me incomprehensible advice whilst I, for my part, was doing my best to loose it by letting the line go slack. It nearly gave my adviser a fit of apoplexy. In the end, and in spite of all my efforts, the dolphin lay panting in the bottom of the boat, its eyes filled with sadness whilst its brilliant colours grew dimmer and dimmer, like footlights in a theatre going out one by one. I have never been big-game fishing again in those waters for fear of catching another one.

Sometimes when you are out hand-lining, you strike a blank patch when the sea seems suddenly empty of fish. Then there is nothing to do but to patrol backwards and forwards in the boat in the hope of picking up the shoals again. The surest guide to the whereabouts of the big shoals are the gulls. You will see them suddenly stop their aimless gliding and hurry to one spot to start diving excitedly into the water. They have spotted their favourite food, the sand eels, who in turn have been forced to the surface by a school of feeding mackerel. As the sand eels splutter along the surface to avoid one fate they find themselves between Scylla and Charybdis, dive-bombed from above and torpedoed from below. Then every boat in the vicinity rushes to the spot until the whole area is seething with activity.

Quite often Charles would come with us on our fishing expeditions and sit goggle-eyed in the bow of the boat watching the fish being pulled aboard. On the whole, however, his favourite sea-going expeditions were on the lobster boats. Although he was scarcely three he soon found his 'sea-legs' and would spend his time rushing from side to side of the boat to see what was going on. It was not long before he learned the difference between the lobsters and the crabs and other shellfish which got into the creels, and would shout with delight when a lobster was brought aboard.

Lobster fishing on the Island has never been in a more prosperous state. There are few people on the Island who do not benefit in one way or another from the obliging lobster. The crofters reap a steady income from them in the summer months and anybody is at liberty to take a stroll amongst the rocks at low tide to catch a few lobsters, which he can turn into hard cash

134

with one of the agents on the Island, or simply provide his family with a good meal at no cost.

The pessimists continue to insist that the lobster is becoming fished out, for fishermen, like farmers, are apt to be born pessimists. In fact the annual catches are becoming steadily greater. This is certainly partly because the men with the big boats like Bill Stout are now fishing lobsters in much deeper water than was ever done before. The lobsters they catch tend to be bigger than the inshore ones. There is a view that they are catching the future breeding stock to the ultimate detriment of the trade, but again the experts say that this is not the case. In fact, the large lobsters that they catch are probably cannibals which do more harm alive on the bottom of the sea than when gracing some gourmet's table.

There are other fishermen who grumble that the summer fishing of lobsters should be stopped and that a close season should be declared as is done in most other parts of the world. During the summer when the lobsters start to come inshore to change their shells, they are generally out of condition and fetch a low price on the market. There is, however, a good reason for allowing the summer fishing of lobsters to continue. The inshore lobsters are fished, for the most part, by the crofter and make an important contribution towards balancing his budget for the year. He hauls his few pots by hand and all he needs is a small rowing-boat, for the pots are set in shallow water so, although the price of the lobsters is low, he has no overheads to set against it.

On the west coast of Scotland there are schemes to store live lobsters in specially constructed reservoirs, kept fresh by the coming in of the tide. In this way they can be re-fished and marketed when the price improves. There are no similar plans yet for the northern isles but perhaps something will be done about it in the future.

A much more nefarious practice amongst lobster fishermen than inshore fishing, it seems to me, is the keeping of the female lobsters when they are spawning. It is, of course, illegal, but you might as well ask a lobster fisherman to throw a pound note into the sea as return a spawning lobster. The evidence in the form of the roe is easily removed, and part of the equipment of every lobster-boat is a stiff-bristled scrubbing brush!

The bigger boats are now equipped to handle more creels than was ever possible before – perhaps as many as a couple of hundred, which are raised from the sea bed, twenty or so on each rope, by a powered winch. It is a great excitement to lean over the gunwale of a lobster boat peering into the depths to be the first to see whether the next pot is occupied or not. Sometimes there are two or even more in a pot and sometimes, for no explicable reason, pot after pot is hauled aboard with none at all.

Often, too, all manner of other strange creatures find their way into the creels. Oddly enough great quantities of shells like buckies manage to crawl in through the aperture and sometimes a four-foot conger eel is found curled up tightly in the pot. Then you have to watch out as it slithers on the deck, for the conger can give a vicious bite. It also makes a strange barking noise like a dog when it is brought out of the water but, in this case, its bite is much worse than its bark.

Most common of all to find in the pots are the ubiquitous crabs. This is another very marketable product for which no market exists amongst the northern isles in spite of the hundred-weights which are caught on each lobster trip. The main reason for this is that they cannot be stored together like lobsters during the shipment to market. When lobsters are placed in their storage boxes their claws are bound with elastic bands so that they cannot attack and damage one another. With crabs this is not possible, so that all that would arrive at the other end would be one or two rather exhausted live crabs and a lot of dead ones. Perhaps if someone would start a crabmeat factory on the Island as has been done in other parts of the country, it would reap a modest fortune.

Although we spent many happy hours lobster fishing, it was under ideal conditions. It is not by any means a leisurely way of making a living for the professional. Whilst a trip on a lobster boat on a quiet warm evening is a pleasant occupation, the job of hauling, emptying and rebaiting the pots in an icy wind is an unenviable task, and the cost of running one of the bigger boats and keeping the pots repaired makes a tidy hole in the profits. Just the same, the price of lobsters is going up and up and is making the trade a much more worthwhile one than it was in the past.

Rich though they are, nobody would claim that the Orkney waters are easy to fish. Apart from the stormy weather of the winter months, there are the rip tides which have to be contended with all the year round. The waters which race through the straits between the islands are always treacherous and the way the tide is flowing dictates the coming and going of the fishing-boats.

Another of the weather factors for which no one can legislate in the Island waters is fog. It appears suddenly and without the slightest warning, blotting out every landmark. Sometimes when you are on the land you can see it being borne in from the open sea like a layer of cotton wool laid on top of the water. These remarkably dense fogs are caused by the cold air meeting the warm water of the Gulf Stream and are often only a thin layer of perhaps twenty feet clinging closely to the surface.

I can remember the fog coming down one afternoon when I was out fishing with Archie Reid by Borough Head. We had intended to have just one run with the net before teatime, to get enough fish to bait the lobster pots. It had been a lovely afternoon with the calm, oily sea scarcely breaking where it lapped against the jagged rocks. Archie had put out his marker buoy and was circling slowly back to it while I sat idly in the bows watching the birds on the cliffs through my field glasses. As he completed the manoeuvre I went aft to stand by the winch as it started to wind in the net.

When I looked back at the headland it had completely disappeared although we could have been hardly a hundred yards from the shore and, by the time the net was in-board, the fog had come down so thickly that you could scarcely see the bows of the boat from the wheelhouse. It was an extraordinary and rather frightening experience to be cut off from the world with such finality. It was just like being in a tiny, grey-curtained room from which there was no escape.

We were only about six miles from harbour but it was late in the evening before we had crept home with Archie feeling his way with the aid of the echo sounder as close into the shore as he dared. In the old days a fisherman caught in a similar predicament would have had to drop anchor and probably spend the night there until the fog had lifted, although, before the modern instruments were invented, I believe a few really expert seamen could judge their nearness to the shore by the pitch of the swell and steer their boats home by this sixth sense.

II. Whales and other Sea Monsters

I am an unreserved believer in sea monsters or sea serpents or call them what you will. There seems to me to be far too much evidence over the years, from completely independent sources, for the reports of the sighting of monsters to be put down to fantasy or optical illusion.

Even in this modern age there are parts of the earth's surface which are still imperfectly known and explored. Our knowledge of the deep and mysterious places of the great oceans is even less complete. The discovery that a fish like the Coelacanth, considered to have been extinct for countless ages, still exists, is only one pointer to the limits of our knowledge. To believe that there are no great monsters yet to be dredged up from the depths is unimaginative in the extreme, even without the evidence of the eye witnesses who claim to have seen them.

Because of this weakness I have for sea monsters I paid more than usual attention when one day, out with a small boat at Borough Head, someone remarked that 'it was just about here that they saw the sea serpent'.

Of course, from the matter-of-fact way it was said, it sounded as if the sighting had taken place within the last few years. When I did some research into the matter I found that it was a well-documented story but that it had happened in the early years of the last century.

It is none the less an interesting story and the similarity it bears to the detail of more recent accounts makes it all the more credible.

In this case two fishermen were just about to pack up for the evening when, thirty yards away from them on the seaward side a huge body rose silently out of the water. At first there was only a small head on a long neck to be seen. Then, as they watched, another great coil of its body came into view until it formed an arch 'large enough for us to sail our boat under'. When they had collected their wits about them they made as rapidly as they could for the shore until, on looking back, they found that the monster had sunk again beneath the waves. When they got back to the village and told their story they came in for a good deal of leg-pulling and some pointed advice about taking more water with it next time.

On the following day, however, another boat was fishing in the same place when the monster obliged with a second appearance. The two fishermen who saw it this time had been amongst the most sceptical, but they were able to confirm the description in every detail except that on this occasion they only saw its head, neck and back before it disappeared.

The report of one coil rising clear out of the water is, I think, unique. On the other hand most reported sightings of monsters describe the small head and a large, bulky body sometimes with paddle-shaped fore-flippers.

I would be less inclined to believe the very considerable evidence which has been amassed on the subject by monster enthusiasts if it were not for an account which I have had at first hand from my cousin Bill Hutchison who still lives overlooking Kirkwall Bay.

Bill has spent many years at sea and, like many of the islanders, has travelled and worked in some strange corners of the world. A more straightforward, down-to-earth character it would be hard to imagine, and certainly not the sort of man whose word anyone would be inclined to doubt.

It happened just before the Great War when he and his father and my Uncle Douglas decided to take their boat over to the Skerries of Work to shoot duck and plover.

Here is Cousin Bill's own account of what he saw, which is also quoted in Tim Dinsdale's fascinaitng and convincing book, *The Loch Ness Monster*:

'We had a twelve-bore shotgun and a Marten-Hendry rifle

aboard, which fired a heavy bullet. We rounded the Head of Holland and had got about halfway between the north point of the Head and the Skerries of Work, when we saw a school of whales heading out in a line just outside our course – leaping clear of the sea, until we could see the Shapinsay land beneath their bellies. The sea stood up in spray as they crashed down on the surface, and we watched them until they were about a mile from us, when they disappeared. We were afraid they might turn and crash down on our boat.

'My father was steering, and after the whales had disappeared, looked ahead for the course for the Skerries – and then I heard him say "My God, boys, what's that?" pointing ahead. I looked up and saw a creature standing straight up out of the sea – with a snake-like neck and a head like a horse or a camel!

'My father turned the boat to port, to make for land and shallow water, bringing the creature abeam. I jumped for the rifle, which was loaded, under the deck, but I heard my father whisper, "Don't shoot, Bill, you might wound it and it'll sink the boat." We all sat silent; I was holding the rifle, intending to make a fight of it if the creature attacked us. The wind was light, and we were leaving the monster quickly. I reckon we sat watching it for about five minutes, when it very slowly began to sink, straight down in the sea, and the water closed over its head without any splash. We now expected it to attack, as we were sure it had been chasing the whales; but we got into shallow water and did not see it again.

'Distances are deceptive at sea, but I reckon we would have been no more than 100–150 yards from the animal. We all three estimated that its head would have been *at least* 18 feet above the surface. My first impression was that it looked as though someone had pushed an enormous tangle above the sea, substituting a horse's head for the leaves of the tangle. It appeared to be dark brown colour, which is the colour of tangle, with lighter stripes running across which could have been caused by the wetness of the neck, which was like a snake; gradually thickening towards the sea's surface, where it would have been about the size of a big man or larger. All three of us were of the opinion that we had seen a sea serpent, and this was my opinion until I later saw the Deepdale Monster.

'Although I have spent a lifetime at sea, I have never seen whales jumping as they did; nor seen a creature like this one. Whalemen know that whales will jump out of the water to get

140

away from Killer whales, and for this reason I think that this creature was following them up, either to attack or from curiosity, when we came on the scene. The whales would have been from 50–60 feet in length and I think one stroke from their tail would have broken the animal's neck.'

Cousin Bill's reference to the Deepdale Monster refers to a strange sea beast which was washed-up in 1941, during the last war. Inspector Cheyne of the Kirkwall Police who took careful tape measurements at the time describes it as follows:

'From head to tail it is 24 ft 8 inches long but it must have been larger than that because part of the head is torn away and some of the tail appears to be broken off.

'The hair on the body resembles coconut fibre in texture and colour. The monster has a head like a cow, only flatter. The eye sockets are three inches in diameter and very deep. The neck, which is triangular, is 10 ft long and 2 ft round, and at the base of the neck there is a bone, shaped like a horse collar and about 4 ft thick. Across the back it has a fin which is 10 inches thick at the base and tapers. This fin is two feet six inches high.

Four flappers with bone structures like hands, each 3 ft 8 inches long were apparently the monster's means of propulsion. The tail is pointed. There is at least a ton of flesh still on the body.'

My brother and I were at school near Inverness and as a great treat at half term we used to be taken to picnic by the side of Loch Ness and peer into its murky depths in the hope of catching a glimpse of 'Nessie', as the monster was christened by sceptical newspaper editors of the day.

We never saw anything, but boys at the Roman Catholic school at Fort Augustus whom we used to play against at various games claimed to have seen it, and the monks believed in it to a man, from the Abbot downwards.

Certainly of all the Scottish lochs, Loch Ness is one of the most sinister. There were wonderful stories told about it which, as schoolboys, we believed implicitly. One was that whenever there was an earthquake in Spain the level of the loch would rise a foot, thus proving beyond all doubt that it was linked with the Iberian peninsula by a subterranean tunnel. Another was that a lady had been out boating on the loch when she fell in and was drowned. She was wearing an immensely valuable pearl

141

necklace and the insurance company employed a diver to recover it. He had no sooner gone down than he signalled violently to be pulled up again. He reported seeing great eels eyeing him from between deep shelves of rock which went back far into the hillside, and insisted that he would not go down again for a king's ransom.

'Nessie' eventually became a national joke and the subject of a flourishing local postcard trade depicting her doing everything from making off with whole sheep in her mouth to blowing the bagpipes. She became the butt of every hoaxer from the one who made mysterious footprints on the loch side with a stuffed elephant's foot to the spoof photographers, and the existence of the monster was thoroughly discredited.

In the last few years, however, there have been several properly fitted-out observation parties who have amassed too much evidence to be discounted. I for one am convinced that the monster seen off the Island, Cousin Bill's monster and 'Nessie' are all members of the same mysterious monster family.

What price the five-foot larva! If a three-inch larva grows into a three-foot eel, a five-foot larva might well produce sixty foot of sea serpent!

Of the known monsters of the sea, the whales are the most breathtaking. Their very bulk makes them fascinating; it is impossible to watch a school of these great creatures plunging out in the bay without a thrill of excitement.

In the old days the islanders used to hunt the schools of whales in small boats – not to harpoon them but to drive them into the shallow waters where they could be easily slaughtered. These were the bottle-nose whales which are now rarely seen around the islands. They were also known as pilot whales because of their habit of following their appointed pilot, if need be right on to the shore.

There was no better place for trapping whales than Rothiesholm Bay near our old house. Sitting on Torness Point, looking down on to the shelving sands Father used to regale us with stories of the old whale hunts until we could almost hear the clamour and the splashing from the boats as they edged a great herd of perhaps a hundred or a hundred and fifty whales on to the shore and see the water running red with blood as the shore watchers fell on the giants in the shallow water with harpoons and even pitchforks. I don't know whether Father himself had

142

ever seen a whale hunt. I think it is unlikely, but his descriptions were satisfyingly graphic and filled with gory details.

The revenue from a big catch of whales could be as much as £500, which was enormous money for the islanders in those days. In addition there would be meat for months to come. They even fed whale meat to the cattle, who ate it with every evidence of enjoyment. The last whale hunt of any size on the Island took place at the end of the last century. Here is an eye-witness account of it.*

'The manse garden commanded a fine view of Mill Bay, and on rushing out into the open air we saw a dark line of boats, some with sails and some with oars, stretching across the blue waters of the broad voe, upwards of a mile from the shore. The practised eye of my host caught the gleam of the dorsal fins in front of the boats, and we immediately hurried down to the beach, scarcely drawing breath till we stood on the bank above the sands of Mill Bay. The inmates of the neighbouring cottages had already assembled in eager groups on the grassy downs, and the other islanders still came flocking from the remoter farms and cabins to the shore. Several of the men were armed with harpoons, while farm lads flourished over their shoulders formidable three-pronged "graips" and long-hafted hayforks.

'Many of the matrons had their heads encased in woollen "buities" and this peculiar headdress imparted a singular picturesqueness to the excited groups on the sea-bank. Other boats with skilled hands on board put off from various points along the shore, and the fleet of small craft in the bay was rapidly increased by the arrival of fresh yawls. The crowd of urchins on the beach, who "thee'd" and "thou'd" each other like little Quakers in the Orcadian vernacular, cheered lustily as boat after boat hove into view around the headlands, swelling the fleet of whalers.

'The line of boats was now little more than a quarter of a mile from the beach. The bottle-nosed or caa-ing whales, showing their snouts and dorsal fins at intervals, seemed to advance slowly, throwing out skirmishers and cautiously feeling their way. As the beach was smooth and sandy, with a gentle slope, the boatmen in pursuit were endeavouring to drive the school into the shallows where harpoons, hayforks and other weapons could be used to advantage.

* From *Summers and Winters in the Orkneys*, by Daniel Gorrie (Hodder & Stoughton, London 1868).

143

'The excitement of the spectators increased as the long line of the sea monsters drew closer inshore. From the boats there came wafted across the water the sound of beating pitchers and rattling rowlocks, and the hoarse chorus of shouting voices. This babel of noises which the water mellowed into a wild war-chant with cymbal accompaniment, was meant to scare the school and hasten the stranding of the whales. But an incident occurred that changed the promising aspect of affairs, turned the tide of battle, and gave new animation to the scene.

'Eager to participate in the slaughter, two or three farm lads, whose movements had escaped notice, suddenly shot off from the shore in a skiff, rowing right in front of the advancing line. The glitter and splash of oars alarmed the leaders and the entire school, seized with a sudden panic, wheeled round and crashed at headlong speed into the line of pursuing boats.

'A shout rose from the shore as the flash of tail fins, the heaving of the boats, and the rapid strokes of the boatmen showed all too plainly the escape of the whales and the success of their victorious charge. Away beyond the broken line of the fleet they plunged in wild stampede, striking the blue waters into spangles of silver foam. Arches of spray, blown into the air at wide distances apart, served to indicate the size of the school and the speed of the fugitives.

'We immediately set off in the direction of Odness to catch a sight of the whales which had quite disappeared from the bay. The boats had turned in pursuit when the school had escaped and they were now making all haste to double the headland. On gaining the top of the cliffs we were glad to see that the whales, recovered from their flight, drifted leisurely along the coast, giving way at times to eccentric gambols.

'Rounding the point of Torness, and stretching across the mouth of (Rothiesholm) bay, the fleet of small craft again hove into view and pressed upon the rear of the slowly advancing and imprisoned whales. Among the onlookers there was now intense excitement, the greatest anxiety being manifested lest the detached wing should follow the main army and again break the line of boats in a victorious charge. The shouting and the noise of the boatmen recommenced and echoed from shore to shore of the beautiful secluded bay. A fresh alarm seized the monsters, but instead of wheeling about and rushing off to the open sea as before, they dashed rapidly forwards a few yards, pursued by the boats and were soon floundering helplessly in the shallows.

'The scene that ensued was of the most exciting description. Fast and furious the boatmen struck and stabbed to right and left; while the people on the shore, forming an auxiliary force, dashed down to assist the massacre, wielding all sorts of weapons. The wounded monsters lashed about with their tails, imperilling life and limb and the ruddy hue of the water along the stretch of shore soon indicated the extent of the carnage. Some of the larger whales displayed great tenacity of life; but the unequal conflict closed at last, and no fewer than a hundred and seventy carcasses were dragged up on the beach.

'The carcasses, as I was told, would realise between £300 and £400; and grateful were the people that Providence had remembered the island of Stronsay by sending them a wonderful windfall of bottle-noses fresh from the confines of the Arctic.'

The writer's last paragraph, expressing devout thanks to God, is reminiscent of the minister from the neighbouring island of Sanday whose Sunday prayer was alleged to end: 'If it be Thy will that ships should run upon the rocks, we pray Thee Lord in Thy Goodness not to forget Thy humble servants on Sanday.'

The caa'ing whale, who gets his name from the word caa, meaning to drive, which is used both in Scotland and on the islands, is now much rarer than it used to be around the islands. They have changed their habits in the last fifty years and now are only found in any number farther north.

Around the Faroe Islands in particular they still appear sufficiently regular for the famous Faroese grindadrap – the whale slaughter – to be a regular occurrence. Indeed the caa'ing whale on the Faroes plays an important part in their economy and the ritual of the whale drive is still preserved in exactly the same form that it has taken for the last five hundred years. At the magic cry of 'Grindabod!' all work on the island ceases on the instant and the whole able-bodied population rush to their boats to take part. The only modern note in the proceedings is that the telephone has taken the place of the fiery cross as the method of alerting the islanders. In front of the Faroese telephone directory pride of place in the instructions on how to make an emergency call is given to the emergency of the Grindabod.

I am indebted to Kenneth Williamson for the following amusing story of a famous 'grind' which he described in his book *The Atlantic Islands* and which took place just before the last war:

One day the men of Hvalbøur were away helping with a minor 'grind' in another fiord and the village was left to the old men, the women and children. Suddenly the cry of 'Grindabod!' was raised and those left behind took to the remaining boats almost to a woman. In great style the Amazons drove a huge school into the bay and set about their slaughter. When their menfolk returned, they found a thousand whales lying dead on the Hvalbøur shore.

There is an odd tailpiece to the story of whales on the Island. Just over ten years ago a school of caa'ing whales were seen heading for Rothiesholm Bay, which was the scene of the last slaughter already described and which has the reputation of being the best whale-trap in all the islands.

The day had long since passed when there was any organisation to deal with such an emergency. The lack of hunters, however, did nothing to deter the whales. They swam steadily inshore and finally beached themselves on the gently shelving sand. What would have been regarded by the islanders of fifty years ago as indeed an act of Providence, now only had nuisance value. By dint of manpower they pulled the smaller whales out to sea again, only for them to swim back on to the beach to rejoin the school. The bigger whales, out of their element, soon suffocated, crushed to death by their own weight. Appeals to Norwegian whale hunters to help themselves to the hundred whales came too late and eventually the carcasses had to be towed out to be dumped in deep water.

There is no explanation for this extraordinary happening unless the guide whale of the school, which all the rest follow, had suddenly become bereft of its sense of direction and led the rest of them to their destruction. Or could it be that Cousin Bill's monster was lurking out in the bay and the whales chose the less fearsome of two fates?

12. Island Retreat

And so the summer drifted past. The book I was working on was nearly finished but we had come no nearer to a decision to leave the Island.

Occasionally a letter from London about work which should be being planned for the autumn would stir my conscience, but it was only a passing twinge. There was always tomorrow to make far-reaching decisions and each day brought its own pre-occupations. When I did finally make a decision to break the even tenor of our existence, it had nothing to do with the admonitions and promptings of agents and publishers in the south.

Ever since our trip to Sule Skerry I had become more and more fascinated by the thought of the many deserted islands which abound in the Orkney Isles. There are in fact almost a hundred islands of which scarcely twenty are inhabited. On several of the smaller islands only one or two families live and, with the passing of the years, the tendency has been for more and more of them to be left to the wind and the sea.

Many of these abandoned islands are used for grazing sheep and support flocks all the year round. For the most part these flocks are left to look after themselves and are only visited regularly during the lambing season. Not long ago a farmer tried the same experiment with cattle. He left them for a couple of years entirely to their own devices, observing them only from time to time with the aid of field glasses from his farmhouse window to see that they were coming to no harm. When he finally went to take off some of the young stock which had bred there, he found that the whole herd had reverted to the wild state and he was lucky to get off again with his life. In the end they all had to be shot with rifles as nobody could do anything with them.

A few years ago John Dennison had bought one of these outlying islands. It was a delightful place which, like Sule Skerry, had once had a manned lighthouse. Now the light was automatic and apart from tending the sheep and a monthly visit to see that the lighthouse was in good working order, nobody ever went there.

I went over with John on one of these trips and was so enchanted by its loneliness that I decided I would make the experiment of going to live there on my own. At least, in my first enthusiasm, I planned to move there *en famille* and live like some Swiss Family Robinson for a few weeks. For once, however, I failed to convert Diana. The idea of weathering out the storms with her and Charles subsisting on what I could catch or shoot did not, for some reason, appeal to her.

As the weather was breaking and bad weather can completely isolate the island, I supposed her view was understandable, but her unexpected resistance made me all the more determined to go through with my plan on my own. So it came about that Mist and I turned up on the pier one fine morning, feeling not a little heroic at the thought of the hardships we were to endure and already enjoying in anticipation the satisfaction we would feel at surmounting them.

The feeling was short-lived. John took one look at the piles of luggage I had heaped on the quay-side and gave a sarcastic snort. 'Is it a three-month safari in unexplored jungle you are setting out on?' he asked.

The extent of my baggage was indeed somewhat shaming. There were sleeping-bags and blankets, an inflatable mattress, a Primus stove and oil lamps. There was a typewriter and piles of reference books. There were guns and rods and cameras, jackets and boots and mackintoshes. Most to be deplored, there was a tea chest so filled with tinned foods of every description that it was almost impossible for one man to load it on to the boat.

I had some idea of demonstrating, during my sojourn, how easy it was to live off the land. After all that was how our ancestors had lived, so why not I? Then I had persuaded myself that it would not be to sybaritic to take a package of tea, which of course meant a kettle and a teapot as well; then a few potatoes and a pot to cook them in and so the rot had set in. I'd finally got loose behind the counter of Willie's shop and piled in two of everything I could think of, Noah's Ark fashion, for use, of course, 'only in an emergency'.

Only in my choice of literature had I finally shown any restraint. I had taken with me the first two volumes of *Das Kapital*. This choice of bedside reading was masochistic more than anything else. I have tried to read *Das Kapital* several times and never got very much further than the first chapter on Commodities which has always proved a barrier to the rest of the work. As it is the ideological handbook for almost as many human beings as read the Bible I have always been rather ashamed of my lack of perseverence. I am unable to go to sleep under normal circumstances without a liberal dose of reading matter so I felt that, if I was ever going to come to terms with Marx, it would be now whilst I was the Dictator of all I surveyed and was able, by a single act of will, to banish all other literature from my realm.

The lighthouse stands at one corner of the island with a substantial little jetty alongside it which makes an excellent harbourage when the wind is set in the right direction. Down at the other end on the seashore there is a small stone bothy which had been built in the old days for the convenience of the kelpers when they came over from the Island in the spring to collect the tangles.

It was hard work portaging my film-star quantity of luggage from one side of the island to the other – a distance of about three-quarters of a mile over rough ground. When I arrived with the first load I had a considerable shock. I pushed open the decrepit door of the hut to discover to my amazement that I had been forestalled. Inside the hut was all the evidence of occupation. The remains of a meal was set out on the rough table, sleeping-bags lay on the floor and there were clothes and articles of equipment everywhere. No Robinson Crusoe could have been more surprised than I was. In an instant my brave picture of myself as the hardy and lonely pioneer lay shattered.

On the way back to the lighthouse I met my fellow hermits. They were two bird-watchers from the Mainland who had been staying a couple of nights to study the migratory birds which call in on the island, and to make a conscientious inventory of the indigenous bird population. I knew one of them by name. He was Eddie Balfour, a well-known bird expert in the Orkneys whose notes on bird life I had often enjoyed in the local paper. Just then it was hard to tell which of us was the more disgusted at seeing the other. On the whole, however, my indignation at having my solitary estate usurped was probably less than Eddie's

149

at finding a stranger armed to the teeth and with a golden labrador at his heels who, so far as he knew, might be planning to make his bird paradise hideous with the sound of gun-fire.

There was worse to come for, I learned from Eddie, there was another visitor expected to the island and a woman at that! She arrived in a fishing-boat that afternoon. She was another well-known Orkney naturalist, Miss Bullard, whose speciality was plant life. When she had pitched her tent in the lee of the light-house wall I began to feel I might as well have retreated to Brighton, so populated had the island suddenly become!

In fact we all settled-in comfortably enough, reconciled to one another's presence, no doubt by the knowledge that they were due to leave again the following day. In fact, as it turned out, the sea proved too rough for the boat to come for them so it was not until the day after that they all finally left, by which time we had got quite used to one another. I was indeed extremely glad to have a chance to talk to Eddie about birds, for his knowledge is vast. When they were comparing notes on the birds they had seen during the day I was quite astonished at the immense variety. Where I would have noticed perhaps a dozen species they discovered a total of over thirty. Only when they came to discuss the number of game birds like snipe and duck did I notice them casting slightly anxious glances in my direction. Out of consideration I did not take my 12-bore out of its case whilst they were on the island.

Pleasant companions though they were I was still glad when I could spread myself in the little cabin and start ordering the routine of my dail existence.

When I had put my cabin in order, my first act was to walk round the whole coastline of my preserve. It took just under three-quarters of an hour, allowing for gazing-out-to-sea time.

Even such a small island has its own history of excitements both old and new. During the last war it saved the life of one of the luckiest pilots in the R.A.F. In dense fog with all his instru-ments shot away, he resigned himself to ditching his aircraft and dropped out of the sky bang into the middle of the island, land-ing on the only flat piece of ground it possesses and missing an ancient standing stone by a matter of inches. When the light-house keeper loomed up out of the fog wearing his high-peaked cap, the pilot, unable to believe his good luck, stumbled out of the plane with his hands up shouting 'Kamerad!'

A grave below the lighthouse tells a story with a less happy ending. Some years ago two farmers on the Mainland fell in love with the same girl. One of them, to improve his chances, murdered his rival, tied him up in a sack and threw him into the sea; but murder will out and the sack was duly cast up on the shore of the island where the victim now lies buried. Inside the sack was the murder weapon which conveniently bore the initials of the murderer. As the dénouement of a plot for a murder story it is too improbable for the most brazen of fiction writers.

The real interest of the island lies in the evidence to be seen on all sides of earlier races who lived there as long as three thousand years ago. Living alone on the island somehow brought those earlier days much closer in time. There is a grass-covered mound which is, in all likelihood, the site of a Stone Age tomb and, in the centre of the island, there are two great standing stones, one broken off half-way up, which pose an everlasting question for the archaeologists.

In its later history there is the story of a sailor, shipwrecked on the island, who had pledged himself that, if he came safely to land, he would build a chapel wherever he came ashore in thanksgiving for his deliverance. There are distinct remains of what, long before living memory, may have been a Christian chapel and alongside it a graveyard which suggests that it may at one time have been a retreat for the Culdee monks.

The days on the island soon started to fall into a pattern. I took to rising with the sun and to shutting myself into the cabin when night fell. Although there were almost twelve hours of daylight it never seemed quite long enough for all the things I wanted to do. One of the most time-consuming of activities was watching the seals.

The pups of the Common Seal looked quite well grown as they lay out on the rocks with their mothers. Amongst them were the big Grey Seals whose breeding-time was drawing near. As the time for their pupping approaches they like to spend most of their time out of the water so that their sleek wet skins become dry and fluffy and they begin to look ludicrously like old ladies lying in the sun in their fur coats.

When I pushed open the door of the cabin each morning the seals, overcome with curiosity, would come swimming in to the shore to get a better view of this strange intruder. When I went down to the shore to wash my plate and mug, their excitement knew no bounds. Sometimes one seal, bobbing its head out of the water a few yards away, would be suddenly surprised by another playfully trying to climb on to its back to get a better view. These antics used to drive Mist to distraction. She would rush furiously into the sea after them and suffer agonies of frustration when they dived below the waves only to pop up again immediately a little farther out to sea.

In order to get my dinner for the evening, I would set off along the shore at first light to see if there were any duck on the little lochan about half a mile away, close to the shore's edge. This manoeuvre delighted the seals who would swim alongside me for all the world like an aquatic pack of fox-hounds. They collected other seals on the way until there were perhaps a hundred of them paddling along contentedly. The noise of the gun did nothing to disturb them although, oddly enough, when I pointed my camera at them they would take immediate fright, all diving together in a boil of spray. If I took the overland route back to the cabin, it was always to find that they had got there first, keeping a close eye on the cabin door to watch for further developments.

There were jagged skerries about a hundred yards offshore from the hut which started to appear as soon as the tide began to ebb. It was the seals' favourite sport to dive and tumble in the dangerous water until enough rock was uncovered for them to haul out on and go to sleep.

At the other end of the island the cliff face has slipped sideways into the sea forming great flat plains of rock where the seals lay and basked all day long. You could creep up on them under cover of the deep fissures carved by the sea, until you were only a few feet from them. Their surprise when you confronted them was delightful to watch. Sometimes they lay staring at you incredulously for a minute or more; then one of them sounded a warning note and they all beat a floppy, ungainly retreat to the safey of the water.

It was, however, at night that the seals were at their most dramatic. Out on the skerries first one started to sing and then another until the darkness was filled with their ululations. The chorus rose and fell with the sade cadences of a love chant, mournful and yet with an unforgettable lilt. It was easy to understand why there is an old belief on the Island that the souls of the dead enter into the seals. Their limpid brown eyes and disembodied crooning had in them all the wistfulness of everlasting regrets.

Breakfast on the island presented few problems. My routine used to be to put the kettle on then walk out on to the rocks with a bamboo pole to which was attached about ten feet of line and three hooks dressed with a wisp of feather. It is a form of fishing which owes nothing to artistry. The method I used and which Eddie Balfour had taught me, was to plunge the whole rod into the deep water off the rocks, reaching down to as near the bottom as possible. Then I would draw the rod through the water in a scything movement and a moment later two or perhaps three fish would be dancing on the hooks. By the time I returned to the cabin with my catch the kettle would have exactly reached the boil. A nice exercise in time-and-motion study.

On the marshy land in the middle of the island, snipe are as common as sparrows. The snipe is not only a delicacy amongst game birds but it has the great advantage for the bachelor cook that it is the only game bird which has no stomach and therefore does not have to be cleaned before cooking. A freshly-shot snipe plucked and cooked within the hour is an epicurean dish indeed. Braised in a pot over a log fire with chopped mushrooms it was one of my greatest culinary successes. I did not fare so well with the duck. My one pot was too small to be useful, so I tried, ingeniously I thought, to roast one on a spit over the Primus stove. The charred embers tasted strongly of paraffin and *canard au paraffin* is not a dish I recommend.

Within a few days of being on the island my larder was full and every morning I had a wide choice of what I should have for dinner hanging from the rafters of the hut.

The hanging of game birds is a subject on which I consider myself an expert. Any game bird is at its best eaten on the day it is shot. If they are to be hung they should be hung for as long as possible and certainly for not less than a week. The whole secret of hanging birds is that they should hang by the neck in a place where the wind can get at them – a draughty larder or better still one of those old-fashioned outside larders made of metal gauze. In this way they will keep for months. Lord Lonsdale, the old 'sporting Earl', used to give his agent a brace of grouse for his birthday every year shot on the last day of the season. Grouse shooting ends on the 15th of December. His agent's birthday was on the 20th March and the birds were always in perfect condition.

The worst aspect of solitary living I soon discovered was the amount of time which has to be devoted to domestic affairs. I can now quite understand why confirmed bachelors tend to become houseproud and pernickety. I am myself the most untidy of people, but even I could not bear the squalor which rapidly developed in the cabin if everything was not put back in its right place. Hours spent looking for the pepper only to find that, when

I came to put them on, it had found its way into one of my Wellington boots and many other similar annoyances, convinced me of the necessity of mending my ways. It did seem to result, however, in my spending a quite disproportionate amount of my time ministering to my own comfort.

My cooking took on a sort of rugged grandeur. Unwilling to waste, for example, half a tin of baked beans left over from a previous meal, I would throw it into the pot with whatever was cooking and the remnants of that meal would be added to the next with the result that, as the days went by, I found myself subsisting on a magnificent goulash in which it was difficult to distinguish whether fish, flesh or fowl predominated. When I inadvertently tipped the remains of a tin of a well-known brand of dog food into the mixture, I decided that the system had got out of hand. Then I scrubbed the pot out and started again.

Other tiresome chores were the collecting of driftwood for my fire and fetching fresh water from the only spring on the island which bubbles out of the rock on the south cliff face. On the other hand, after a few days, they became automatic, so that I could busy myself about the routine tasks with my mind elsewhere. Lack of human contact I found exhilarating rather than the reverse. I had no wireless set, so the problems of the world lay lightly on my shoulders.

Under normal circumstances, when I settle down to write, I find that I require at least half an hour to exorcise the immediate problems of day-to-day living from my mind. On the island I realised how much of this 'think time' is taken up with such vital problems as whether to order more coal or profitless ones like whether the Russians have really got a bomb which can wipe out the whole world. On the island I found that I could sit down at my typewriter and start work right away and that I could write for much longer periods without a break. Being a chain-smoker while I am working, I had taken an immense supply of cigarettes; but I found that I had only smoked about half of what I had expected to.

Mist on the other hand did not take to a hermit's existence quite as happily as I had expected. She found the hours lying on the cliff-tops watching the shags with their burnished necks gleaming in the sun distinctly tedious. For the bird lover the island is an inexhaustible pleasure ground, but manx shearwaters and gannets and purple sandpipers and snow buntings meant nothing to her.

She developed another indiosyncrasy which I have never

known in a dog before. After I had shut the door of the cabin at night, nothing would persuade her to leave it again until sunrise. If I went out to listen to the keening of the seals or to catch the soft wing-beats of the migratory birds as they passed over the island, she would only come with me as far as the door and then return to her bed, making little whimpering noises. Yet when we returned home, she took up her old habit of coming for a walk with me every night at bedtime as enthusiastically as ever.

Even stranger; at, so far as I could judge, precisely the same time every evening, she would suddenly spring from her corner and stand with her hackles raised, growling at the door, although I could hear no sound outside which could have excited her. Having registered her protest she would then return to her bed to sleep soundly until morning. Perhaps the murdered farmer was turning in his cold grave by the seashore!

For me almost the best time of all was at night. Then I would go and stand on the cliff-tops and watch the moon rise out of the sea and listen to the little sounds which fill the darkness if you have ears to hear them; the startlingly human sound which the sheep make like a stifled cough, the chuckle of the duck passing overhead and the rustle of unseen life all around.

To stand alone amongst the monuments of the past and let the imagination wander back into the mists of time does not induce a sense of loneliness. Rather it telescopes the pageant of history and brings it into focus. Only the busy streets of the big cities seem incredibly remote and unreal, like a strange dream imposed upon the reality of things. In the foreground were the squat figures of the Picts emerging from their underground dwellings to busy themselves with the tasks of the night, for it was at night that the Picts gained strength. With the rising of the sun their powers left them and they retired underground to replenish their spent forces. Closer even than the Picts were the gaunt, wild figures of the Vikings, rowing their high-prowed boats in from the open sea, guided by the same unchanging stars. The crashing of the waves on the rocks might have been the organ refrain to Isaac Watts's great hymn.

> A thousand ages in Thy sight
> Are like an evening gone;
> Short as the watch that ends the night
> Before the rising sun.

When, early one morning, I saw a smudge on the horizon I found myself wishing with all my heart that it would not be

John's boat. Suddenly everything on the little holm seemed immensely familiar as if I had lived there all my life and even the Island to which I was returning did not seem quite as enviable a place as when I had left it.

I suppose the psychologists would say that this discovered love of solitude is only a symptom of an unwillingness to face the stresses of everyday living. I expect they would be right, for most of us suffer from this form of cowardice to a greater or lesser degree, and most religions recognise the value of temporary retreat from the world. Although I cannot say that I found a great deal of time for praying for the sins of the world, I did feel that, in some indefinable way, my own retreat had been worthwhile. It was only when I came to pack up in the hut that I realised that I have still to get past the first chapter of *Das Kapital*.

When I got back to the Island, I discovered that in my absence all manner of epoch-making events had taken place. The cat had had kittens and a General Election had been declared. Everything seemed to have gone swimmingly without me and, for that matter, I had managed pretty well without all of them.

13. Shooting and other Matters

September comes as the crops begin to ripen and the soft dusk starts to fall, almost noticeably earlier each evening. With the beginning of September comes the duck-shooting season when everyone with a gun is to be seen slipping off in the evening to their favourite stand to wait for the mallard coming flighting in to feed.

Shooting on the Island is a very democratic business. There is no preserved land and the duck, snipe, golden plover and rock pigeons are there for anyone who cares to go out after them. It is one of the last places where shooting is free for the asking. At least, I know of nowhere else in England or Scotland except on the tidal waters. I suppose if there were it would soon become so over-shot as to be of no real benefit to anyone, and least of all to the game.

That shooting should be becoming such an expensive and exclusive sport is regrettable. I do not have a solution for this state of affairs, but it remains a pity, for any sport as good as shooting should be enjoyed by as many people as possible. I have very little patience with the lunatic fringe of the anti-blood-sport brigade who, in the same breath, condemn shooting and fishing with fox-hunting and stag-hunting as cruel sports.

Stag-hunting I regard as being indefensible and, indeed, the arguments for fox-hunting put up by fox-hunting people seem to be rather poverty-stricken.

On the other hand I have time for the dyed-in-the-wool fox-hunting man who understands the game, respects other people's rights and makes no absurd excuses for enjoying his sport. More

157

often than not he is an asset to the countryside and a popular fellow. But there I am sticking my neck out about something that doesn't concern me and about which I know precious little.

My main complaint is that the social aspects of hunting seem to be spreading into the sports of fishing and shooting. Nowadays the greatest social cachet is to be obtained by the paying of more and more fantastic prices for salmon beats and grouse moors and pheasant coverts so that they begin to cease to be country sports and become the plaything of people who regard fresh air in any other context as thoroughly undesirable.

On the Island there are no such social considerations, and while there remain no grouse or pheasants or salmon there is little fear of a take-over bid from a tycoon.

Of all the sporting birds on the Island perhaps the most sporting are the rock pigeons. When plucked they are no bigger than a snipe and just as good to eat. Certainly they are just as hard to shoot. From early morning the rock pigeons are out in the fields feeding. Sometimes, when you stop at the side of a corn-field, they rise up like a flock of fluttering moths and then drop back into the corn. In the evening they return in ones and twos to the cathedral-like caves in the cliffs where they roost.

One of the ways of shooting them is to take a boat round the headlands. When you clap your hands, they erupt from their roosting places and hurl themselves twisting and turning out into the sunlight, spiralling up into the air, so that, unless you are uncommonly quick, they are out of range before you have had time to steady yourself in the rocking boat. Sometimes when you fire, the bird you have aimed at, feigning death, will close its wings and drop like a stone to within inches of the water before flattening out and jinking off over the waves. A less speculative method is to stand on the dizzy brink at the top of the cliffs and wait for them to come skimming in from their feeding grounds. My usual companion on these cliff-top adventures is Ralph Fotheringhame, who has the remarkable ability of being able to concentrate on shooting whilst hanging on by his eyebrows above a breathtaking drop of a hundred feet.

There is one place out on the headlands where a fall of rock makes it possible to crouch on the cliff face without too imminent a danger of crashing on to the serrated rocks below. To sit on this small platform is to be in a strange and wonderful world. On one side the cliffs rise in twisted, weather-beaten spires to the sky. On the other side the sea slaps and gurgles below you on the rocks, throwing up every now and again a fine cloud of spray which hangs and glitters in the shafting sunlight. The gulls come gliding round, tipping their wings to peer curiously at you in your eyrie, so close that you can almost reach up and touch them.

Sometimes I got there early, before the pigeons had finished their daily feasting and were ready for home, so that I could sit and watch the cliff slowly come to life. Tiny finches flit about the rocks pecking at the cracks for insects with their sharp beaks. Rock pipits and linnets abound, scurrying to and fro and dancing suddenly into the air. Far out in the bay is the only sign of human life; a fishing-boat ploughing a straight furrow across the cerulean surface of the sea, chugging its way out to beyond the headland to hand-line for mackerel with which to bait the lobster pots; straight below, so close to the rocks that each wave would seem certain to dash them against the face, the cormorants bob together like celluloid toys.

At a distance cormorants are not likable birds. Their saturnine, gloomy appearance is against them. They communicate with each other in a hoarse croak like a death rattle and, in their heavy, purposeful flight, they look like professional mourners on their way to a funeral.

I only changed my mind about them when, one afternoon, I saw a pair of them really close to. I was lying half asleep in the hot afternoon sun in my rocky hide when a male and female cormorant flopped on to a narrow ledge less than two yards away. At once the male started courting his girl friend in the most touching way. With his bill he ruffled her neck feathers and nuzzled her with his head with a show of the most affectionate ardour.

For a time she stood aloof with proper maidenly modesty. Then she started, gently at first but soon passionately, to return his caresses. It was altogether a pretty picture, but when I reached for my camera, the movement disturbed them and they dived together off the ledge into the clear water below, leaving behind them a glittering trail of bubbles coruscating in the sunlight.

The manner in which the pigeons come depends on the direction of the wind and, I believe, on the state of the tide. In this last respect they resemble the rabbits on the Island who keep to their burrows while the tide is out and leave them when the tide is in. Ralph, who may be a first-class shot but has some pretty wild theories, holds the opinion that rabbits behave in this way all over the world and that even in central Australia the rabbits pop in and out of their holes according to the state of the tide on the coast six hundred miles away. In the vividness of his imagination he is only excelled by one of his friends whose stories are apt to start, 'Did I ever tell you about the time I caught a lobster seven feet long . . . ?'

Certainly I have noticed that the pigeons are for some reason reluctant to enter their caves when the tide is in but enter without hesitation when there is a low tide. Sometimes, too, they come over high in the air and dive down suddenly. At others they come skimming fast and low over the cliff-tops, flashing into view and disappearing again in a matter of seconds.

It takes time and a great expenditure of cartridges to become really proficient at the sport, for it is easy enough to fire fifty shots with scarcely enough pigeons to make a pie to show for them.

After shooting pigeons, duck seem ponderous by comparison as they come chuckling in to feed in the gathering dusk. The way of life of the wild duck is the reverse of the pigeons'. They go out at night to feed and return to the open water in the daytime where they are comparatively safe from their enemies. It is in October, when the great migratory flocks of widgeon arrive from the north, that the sport is at its best. With widgeon come other migrating duck and sometimes a sudden invasion of geese resting on their journey to winter on the estuaries and lochs farther south.

At the beginning of the shooting season, Mist was over two years old and I felt that it was time she took life a little more seriously. Retrieving has always been second nature to her as she is constantly at pains to demonstrate by fetching everything from old bones to, on one occasion, a lady's handbag which the unfortunate owner had put down for a moment on the floor of the shop. Mist raced down the street after me with it, scattering powder, lipstick and money as she went.

On her regular training sessions, however, I have the greatest difficulty in persuading her that retrieving an old sock stuffed with straw is a very serious business and not a game I have invented for her amusement. In order to reproduce as nearly as possible actual working conditions, I have a blank cartridge pistol. When this is fired she is expected to sit as steady as a rock until I send her off to find the sock which is hidden near by. She seemed to get the idea in the end, so that by the opening of the shooting season I was confident that she knew enough of the rules to start working in earnest.

On the first evening of the duck shooting I took up my stand

160

at the corner of a cornfield to wait for the duck to come in. Everything went according to plan and the first duck fell dead thirty yards behind me. Mist's behaviour was exemplary. She never moved a muscle until I sent her off for the retrieve. Then she took off like a rocket and kept going. She turned up again twenty minutes later which was the time it had taken her to get to the car and back with the sock in her mouth!

Shooting of any kind is only sport to the extent that it is enjoyable in its performance. Success or failure are of minor importance. By this criterion the flighting of duck must come near the top of the list in the affections of most sportsmen.

A day shooting pheasants where the bag is counted in hundreds is not necessarily a memorable day of sport other than to the statistically minded. I once was invited to a shoot in the south of England where the guns were rushed over the flat, dull countryside in a fleet of Land-Rovers. No sooner was one drive over than we were whirled off again to face another line of beaters, leaving behind an army of camp followers to pick up the dead birds resulting from the last onslaught. The final bag was phenomenal and the agony, for me at any rate, complete. I would have had much more enjoyment condemned to spend the day at a fun-fair, shooting at clay pipes with an air rifle.

I have spent many evenings out duck flighting without ever firing a shot and yet returned refreshed and exhilarated from having watched the sun drop slowly below the horizon and seen the long shadows creep across the fields. Sometimes, if the wind is right and the place you have chosen the correct one, you can have more excitement in half an hour of duck shooting than in a whole day of potting at pheasants.

One night in particular, out of many on the Island, remains in my mind. John Stevenson, one of my farming friends, and I had been out several nights that year with negligible results. The harvest was almost over. Just a few fields remained in stook and the season for the equinoxial gales was not far off. After a long, unnaturally calm day it started to blow from the north and by the time we had taken up our positions along a dry-stone dyke, it was beginning to freshen into a gale.

From where I stood I could see the long breakers rolling into the bay and beyond, on the next headland, the lights were coming on in the farmhouse windows, one by one. This is the magical time, when the night, gradually overtakes the day, which never fails to fill me with wonder. A wall, one moment clearly seen, becomes suddenly blurred and the the next time you look, it is only a long dark, scarcely-seen shadow. It is the hour for strange fancy and heightened perception. You are of the world and yet no part of it, like Voltaire on his ladder looking down on humanity. The warmness of the distant light lends a personal remoteness and sets free the imagination to soar at will over the waste places of the earth. If ever a man doubts the immortality of his soul I would tell him to stand alone at the onset of night and wonder at the majesty of all creation.

When the duck come they come suddenly, looming for a moment against the spent light of the sky to be swallowed up as quickly again in the darkness. On this evening the first two mallard came just as I was beginning to believe that this was to be another blank evening. They passed low over my head before I had time to jerk myself back to reality. A moment later John's gun flashed in the darkness farther down the wall, the noise of the report swept away on the wind so that it sounded like the dull plop of a stone dropped into the water.

Then the duck really started to come. The heavy mallard at first, their wings curving tautly as they plunged against the wind. Then the widgeon with their thin whistling, travelling low in flocks of ten and twenty and so fast that the rush of their wings overhead was like the swish of an express train passing through a tunnel. The moon had risen and still the duck kept on coming, silhouetted against the scudding cloud. For some reason every duck from miles around seemed determined to feed on that field. They were still coming when John materialised out of the dark to say that he was running out of cartridges. When I felt in my bag I had only two left. Just then a single teal came over so high that I would not have wasted shot on it. John killed it stone dead. He has an irritating habit of 'wiping my eye' in this way so that when, a moment later, he missed a mallard which nearly knocked his hat off, I felt mightily pleased that the night had ended for him on such a suitably chastening note.

As we made our way home, splashing down a muddy cart-track, weighed down by the weight of our bag, the wind suddenly dropped and the moon broke clear of the wispy cloud, touching the cornfields with a pale golden light and casting shimmering pathways on the sea to the far horizon where the lighthouse on Copinsay swung its beam from a lonely headland.

'It's been a great night's sport,' I said.

'It would have been a great night without the duck,' said

John. Even the islanders never take the magic of the Island for granted.

When the autumn weather starts to turn stormy and the gale force winds make duck shooting too unpredictable a business, the islanders have a unique way of getting them. The dirtier the night the better; the equipment needed is a powerful torch and a large, strong edition of a butterfly net. The duck, and snipe for that matter, pay no attention when they are caught in the beam of light but the moment the descending net comes into their view they are off quicker than you would imagine possible. You have to have very quick reactions to anticipate which way they will go, but a practised netter will do better than the best gun.

Another sign of the approaching winter is when the tangle men start looking for the south-easterly gales which will bring the seaweed into the Island.

Although the old kelp industry had died with the discovery of new ways of manufacturing iodine, a new industry has now grown in its place. After a number of years when the industry was completely dead, an enterprising company on the west coast of Scotland found new uses for the tangle and bladder-wrack. Now they are in greater demand than ever before. More encouraging still, new uses are constantly being discovered each year for the alginic acid which is the by-product of the tangle. It has a use in the manufacture of such widely different products as ice-cream and emulsion paint, toothpaste, sausage skins and washable wallpaper.

It is now no longer necessary for the tangle farmer to produce his own kelp. All that is required of him is that he should haul up the tangles off the beach during the winter months and leave them to dry on the foreshore. In the spring boats come up from the Hebrides, where the headquarters of the industry is, to collect the result of his labours. So great has the demand become that the price has climbed steadily from £8 per dry ton to almost twice that amount and still there is not enough to satisfy the demand and the search for new sources of supply is now extending as far as Iceland.

In order to encourage the islanders to take part in this new and admirable development, the alginate industry will lend the tangle farmer money so that he can buy a tractor to haul his tangles in greater quantities. They are even enlightened enough to help him to buy a boat, not so much to help him with his tangle farming but to enable him to earn a living in the summer from fishing, and so be able to be independent all the year round, fishing in the summer months and devoting himself to the tangles in the winter.

This policy is now finding a deserved success. The company which started in a small way after the war with the assistance of a few thoughtful Highland lairds, has developed into big business which is constantly putting money back into exploring new fields in which their product can be used. Already their factories are employing considerable numbers in the depopulated areas of the west coast of Scotland and bringing money to the remote island communities. Most encouraging of all, the tangle industry is helping the fast-disappearing race of crofters to continue to survive.

The crofter's life has always been a hard one, but, of all men, I envy his way of life the most. There is no doubt that the Scottish crofter who had to live by his land alone, has gone for ever. The depopulated Highlands bear silent witness in the ruined homesteads which scatter the glens, to the economic impossibility of living off a few bare acres. His life was always a struggle against fearful odds. Today, with the new scientific developments in the farming industry his chance of survival has disappeared altogether.

The Island crofter is however quite a different species. His eggs are by no means all in one basket and there is no reason why the hard-working crofter who takes advantage of his opportunities should not only survive but prosper.

I suppose most of us have, at some time or another, hankered after the simple way of life. The cottage with roses round the door is an attractive image to let the mind's eye rest upon when everything around us in our daily lives looks complex and forbidding. It is, alas, an illusion – an infinitely desirable mirage which, in contemplation, makes life supportable in the arid wastes of the big cities. It has no substance in reality, as most people discover who retire to their dream cottage. Within a few years they are dead from boredom, suffocated by their own inactivity.

The need in the northern isles today is for young and vigorous men with the spirit of independence and the will to work for their own salvation. They are, in fact, the very men whom the young countries like Australia and Canada set out to attract. When I remarked on this to one of the islanders he agreed with me. 'But you must remember that it only costs £10 to emigrate to Australia where it cost almost £30 for a man to come up here!' he added with a twinkle in his eye.

True enough! Just the same it is surprising how many of the best of our young men set out each year determined to make their fortunes far from home and none who consider the opportunities at their own back doors.

I have remarked that the Island crofter has an enviable life and it is true. He is as nearly self-contained as it is possible to be. He produces his own milk and eggs at very little cost and digs his own fuel for nothing from the peat bogs. Each winter the sea delivers the tangle at his front door and each summer his lobster pots provide an income sufficient to provide such luxuries as he requires. His own corn provides the meal which used to be the staple diet of the crofter and to vary it there are rabbits and game and every form of fish from kuithes to haddocks, fresh from the sea or cured by the simple method of salting them and hanging them up on a line to dry. His work is hard but it has the virtue of variety and this is the element surely most lacking in a more sophisticated way of living.

He must, too, be a man of considerable resource with several trades at his fingertips. Not only does he fish on his own account and spend his evenings making his own lobster pots; but he farms his own land and yet always seems to be available to lend an extra pair of hands on the bigger farms during the busy times like the harvesting and the sheep shearing. He must be a contented man within himself, for each succeeding season makes its demands on him and he can seldom take a holiday. Yet his is the most truly independent way of life, and real independence is surely one of the ambitions most to be sought after. Set his life against one of watching the clock until it ticks round to the minute of escape from the desk or the work bench and there can surely be little comparison.

It is surprising to remember that the population of the Island a hundred years ago was in the region of 1,500 people. Today ther are scarcely 500 and yet conditions of living and the general level of prosperity are incomparably higher than at any time in the history of the Island. Even as recently as the years between the wars the standard of living was extremely low. I have often sat with old Magnus Dennison, John Dennison's father, and listened to him talk of his early life when he started work at five in the morning on a breakfast of milk and fresh-baked bread and worked through the day until supper-time at seven with only an hour off at midday for his dinner. In those days a farm lad would get perhaps £10 for the half year and the money paid in arrears at that.

When I was a boy, and if I got up early enough, I could watch the farm hands having their traditional breakfast which was simply raw oatmeal scalded with boiling water. I can remember my mother being horrified at such rough fare and trying to introduce a substantial breakfast of ham and eggs. It almost caused a revolution until they had their brose back again. When I recounted this to Magnus Dennison he said solemnly, 'What I would not give for a plate of brose now, cooled with a drop of home-brew ale. There is no dish like it in the world.'

Now the minimum agricultural wage is over ten pounds a week, with the benefits of the Welfare State in addition. Yet the old men who can remember the bad old days do so with nostalgia, which is in striking contrast to the memories of the men from the industrial areas. Just the same, it was the bad old days which brought about the drift away from the Island. For the younger generation the grass was ever greener over the fence and, indeed, when the time came to spread their wings, the croft was altogether too small a place.

Not so long ago the average land holding on the Island was thirty acres. Now there are fewer but bigger farms and every year there are more crofts where the door has been closed for the last time. Some farms are as big as 300 acres and more. The biggest is 600 with another 400 acres of moorland grazing. This tendency to bigger and bigger farms has altered the problems of economic survival and has made the Island less self-supporting. It is, in fact, the same problem in miniature as faces any country which has a diminishing home market. Markets have to be found for the increasing number of stock being raised through intensive farming, which means sending cattle and sheep perhaps a hundred and fifty miles by sea. The freight is the same for an animal of poor quality as for a good one but only a good one will fetch a high enough price to justify the expense. Island-raised beef must fetch six or seven pounds a head more than Scottish-reared cattle to give the farmer the same return. So the age of the specialist has arrived on the Island. It is only the big farmer with the money to buy-in a top-quality bull who can hope to survive. Even with the highest grade breeding stock he must still be a highly skilled man ready to adopt new ideas and new methods if he is to prosper. Just as he is penalised by having to bear the cost of exporting his cattle he also has to bear the burden of paying higher prices for his feeding stuffs and artificial manures, for he has to import them. That the Island farmers are not only surviving but flourishing is an indication of their high standard of efficiency, reflected in the excellence of their produce.

The emphasis on specialisation also affects the fishermen. There are fewer farmers who are fishermen and fishermen who are farmers. The man who earns his living by the sea must also find a quality market for his products. The lack of a home market and the competition of big modernly equipped boats working directly to the big ports has killed the white-fish industry. The professional fisherman must rely on the luxury market for lobsters and must catch them in sufficient quantities to stand the overheads. This means bigger boats with a longer range of operation manned by a crew who also have their wages to be earned. To equip such a boat means the investment of upwards of £2,000, which is big money.

Yet I do not believe that the day of the crofter is done. There may be a legacy of empty smallholdings scattered over the Island but there remains plenty of sturdy individualists with a small boat and a few acres for whom there are still 'flowers in the garden and meat in the hall'.

14. Goodbye

With the onset of winter we were glad to spend more and more time behind our own front door. The days shortened rapidly so that we got up while it was dark and the lights had to be put one while it was still early afternoon. The harvest had long since been safely stowed away, the sealing season was over and the long, dark, stormy months lay ahead.

The winter, when the inter-island boat makes the trip less frequently and bad weather sometimes cuts the islands off completely, is the testing time for the fishermen. Then the seas turn against them and battle is joined. The North Atlantic Drift pushing its way eastwards across the Atlantic and reinforced by the thrust of the cold waters from Baffin, meets the waves, borne by the strength of the winter gales racing in the opposite direction, and the conflict throws up the waters in torment. It is this phenomenon which accounts for the great roosts off Shetland's Sumburgh Head and which is the cause of the colourfully-named Bore of Duncansby and the Merry Men of Mey which rage at either end of the Pentland Firth.

Even the staid *British Islands Pilot* in describing these waters is stirred out of its usual objectiveness:

In the terrific gales which usually occur four or five times a year all distinction between air and water is lost, the nearest objects are obscured by spray, and everything seems enveloped in a thick smoke; upon the open coast the sea rises at once, and striking the rocky shores rises in foam to several hundred feet and spreads over the whole country.

The sea, however, is not so heavy in the violent gales of short continuance as when an ordinary gale has been blowing for many days; the whole force of the Atlantic is then beating against the shores of the Orkneys, rocks of many tons in weight are lifted from their beds and the roar of the surge is heard for twenty miles; the breakers rise to a height of 60 feet and the broken sea on the North Shoal, which lies 12 miles northwestward of Costa Head is visible at Skail and Birsay . . .

There is always a great deal of disagreement between sailors as to the actual height which the great waves attain. Some contend that they seldom reach higher than thirty feet and only become bigger, like fishermen's tales, in the mind of the beholder. Others believe them to rise in the open ocean to over twice that height. Whatever the truth, when these giant breakers are hurled upon the shore their force is unbelievable. At Wick during the last century the seas carried away a breakwater with an estimated weight of over a thousand tons and five years later battered the new pier weighing 2,600 tons to smithereens.

Perhaps even more awesome is the fact that the wild waters of the Pentland hurling themselves against the 300-foot cliffs at Dunnet Head have broken the windows of the lighthouse which stands above its highest point.

Most sinister of all, and of the most danger to fishermen who ply their trade in these ferocious waters, are the times when the tide from the open Atlantic is setting eastwards, compressing itself between the islands whilst the wind is pushing great lumps of water through in the opposite direction. Then the whole surface of the sea is dotted with strange upward-pushing eruptions and eddying whirlpools which can suck down a man and his boat unlucky enough to get drawn into its clutches. Even in calm weather boats are wise to avoid the Swilkee, as it is known, in the Pentland Firth, and there are many cases of small boats putting out between the islands in fine weather and never arriving at their destination.

The Orkney waters are certainly amongst the most dangerous in the world and, in earlier days, shipwrecks were frequent occurrences. In fact, when an island boat was not involved, shipwrecks were not regarded as calamities by the islanders. Quite the reverse, the poverty on the islands particulary in the winter was so great that a good wreck was looked forward to for the rich pickings it might provide. There were even ghoulish tales of islanders luring ships to their destruction by leading a pony along the cliffside in the darkness with a green light burning to starboard and a red light to port.

One of the strangest trials for witchcraft recorded in the Court records concerns a ship in danger of being wrecked on the island of Westray. The heroine of the story, for heroine she undoubtedly was, was Jane Forsyth, known as the Storm Witch, who was arraigned by the infuriated populace for saving an impressively rich-looking ship from being dashed to pieces on their shore. The whole population were watching with greedy anticipation as the storm-bound vessel swept nearer and nearer to a hidden skerry, when Jane Forsyth pushed her way through the crowd and leaping into her father's boat managed, by a miracle of sea-manship, to reach the vessel. Seizing the wheel she brought it safely into the shelter of the bay.

A later generation would have made a Grace Darling of her but the frustrated islanders declared that only a witch could have overcome such a storm and she was condemned to the stake.

The story, which is a true one, had a dramatic and happy ending. Jane Forsyth, unlike most witches, who were bent and ugly, was an attractive young girl whose heart had been broken when her lover had been snatched from her by the press-gang. In the best story-book fashion the lover returned in the nick of time. As she lay in the condemned cell on the eve of her execution, he contrived to drug the guards and effect her rescue. They fled to, of all places, Manchester, where they set up in business as merchants and, so far as anyone knows, lived happily ever after.

Today in the snug Island harbour the lifeboat rides uneasily at anchor ready to go to the rescue of any boat caught in the turbulent sea and, during the winter, not long elapses before the warning sounds again. Then the crew drop what they are doing and clamber into their yellow oilskins to give battle to the elements while everyone on the Island waits tensely for their return.

It was well on into the autumn when Diana and I reluctantly decided that the time had come when we had to return to take up our life again in London which we had left so many months before. It was not the threat of the wild weather to come which finally drove us to the decision but the plain necessity of earning a living. My book had been long since finished. All the articles which I had promised myself I would write when the opportunity offered, had been sent off to the papers for which they were intended and now what I needed was new ideas and new assignments.

In fact, if it had not been for the necessity of re-establishing contacts and planning the work for the following year, nothing would have suited us better than to remain in our snug lodgings, for the winter is a friendly and sociable time on the Island.

The last few days were sad ones as we went the rounds saying goodbye to all the friends whom we had come to know so well. I made a sentimental journey down to the south end of the Island to look once more at Peter's deserted croft where the roof is now beginning to fall in and where, more years ago than I care to remember, I had first heard the stories of the colourful history of the Island I had learned to love so well. We went again to visit the old family house and take tea with Harriet in the familiar room and talk about the past and present in a way which contracted time, and we spent convivial evenings in houses which had become almost as familiar.

One evening in particular stands out. It was almost the last night we were to spend on the Island and I was glad it was such a typical one. There were about a dozen of us crowded into the small room and the half-bottles, as they are apt to do, were passing from hand to hand while we discussed everything from the latest iniquities of the Government to what Bessie said when the minister called and caught her in her curlers.

In time the conversation turned to the ills and injustices which the Island has to endure, for, as I have said, when it comes to having a good grumble the islanders are second to none.

'It's all very well for you,' one of the company said to me accusingly. 'Now that you've got your bit of a book finished, the Island will have seen the last of you!'

'Nonsense!' I said hotly. 'The trouble with you lot is that you do not know when you are well off. Lobster for your supper any night you want it; finest fillet steak at five shillings a pound. More houses than you can make use of, no unemployment problem and if you want money as well – why, you can just go and pick it off the foreshore – '

I'd like to have developed the theme but I was not given the opportunity. 'What about the cost of groceries?' one shouted. 'What about freight rates?' shouted another. 'What sort of a life is it for young folks?' and so on – and on and on.

When the pandemonium had subsided we decided what was

to be done. We would break away from England and her perfidious administration. We would declare Kirkwall a free port. Freed from excise duties, we would sell whisky at six shillings a bottle and cigarettes at eightpence a packet. We would print our own money and our own stamps and sell them to collectors all over the world. We would be the tourists' paradise and the trading Mecca of the north.

Soon we were carving up the Government posts between ourselves. We had a ready-made Minister of Agriculture and an obvious candidate for the Ministry of Fisheries. We had a Home Secretary and a Chancellor of the Exchequer. I thought I had a chance of the Prime Ministership but in pressing my claims too vigorously I nearly finished up as a mere paid official in charge of Public Relations. In the end, however, I managed to obtain the post of Ambassador to the Court of St James. There is no saying where it might all have ended if a very late arrival had not looked in bringing his fiddle with him. Then the lovely dream faded as we sang the old songs and the contents of the half-bottles got lower and lower.

Altogether it had been a grand night of music, conversation and friendship so that the following morning when we boarded the steamer everything seemed more grey by comparison. We stood shivering together on the deck while the car was hoisted aboard and, by dint of much heaving on ropes and shouted advice, was lowered into the hold which it shared with eight black cattle. Mist, who had been content to make the journey to the Mainland locked in the car, barked in furious objection when she saw her travelling companions peering curiously in at the windows. Charles, sensing that this was no ordinary trip to Kirkwall, joined in the protest by bellowing loudly; the steamer blew a blast on her siren, drowning our last shouted goodbyes and we were off.

As we passed the Green Holms, the uninhabited islands which stand in the midst of the turbulent channel which divides the north isles from the Mainland, I could see the Grey Seals still hauled out on the rocks in considerable numbers. For half an hour the steamer tossed and bucked as she ploughed across the tide to gain the shelter of Shapinsay Sound and then we started the long run into Kirkwall Bay.

Kirkwall is a town with two faces. There is the face you see when you first arrive there from the populated areas of the south. Then it seems a small, leisurely town with its squat, grey buildings amounting to little more than a cluster of houses under the dominating shadow of St Magnus Cathedral. The narrow, flag-stoned main street which serves both pedestrians and motorists with seemingly dangerous impartiality, appears at the same time both quaint and foreign so that it is with surprise that one remembers that Kirkwall is the capital of a Scottish county. It would have seemed quite natural to discover that the shopkeepers, in spite of the English goods they sold, only spoke Norwegian.

Arrive in Kirkwall, however, from a spell in the northern isles and the impression gained is quite a different one. It then wears the face of the sophisticate. The houses facing the harbour are impressive palaces, the bustle of the main street is intimidating and the rows of shops bewildering in the variety of goods they have to offer. To stand for a moment at a street corner is to feel conspicuous, so purposefully does everyone appear to be going about their business.

We decided to linger a few days on the Mainland to see old friends and find our land legs, as it were, before adventuring farther south. We climbed the hill above Kirkwall to see Cousin Bill in the big, grey house where he lives overlooking the town and we made another trip out to see Miss Johnstone, married now these many years to Jackie Shearer who I could only just remember from the long ago days when he came courting her and used to give us sixpences. There were the Storer Cloustons to see in their long-eared house which overlooks Scapa Flow and where Erlend's father wrote the books which made him famous and there was a visit to Stanley Cursitor who has the proud title of the Queen's Limner and lives surrounded by his paintings in a house from which, if you felt so inclined, you could dive out of the drawing-room window into the clear waters of Hoy Sound.

One evening I deserted Diana to attend a dinner at which Jo Grimond was to speak and where I found, after I had arrived and to my great confusion, that I was also expected to perform. Jo is, of course, the Member of Parliament for Orkney and Zetland, and somehow combines the onerous business of serving his remote and scattered constituency with his rôle as Leader of the Liberal Party. He had come to the Island during the General Election to discuss knotty questions like whether one day there would be a landing strip for an air-ambulance service and hardy annuals like what was he going to do about the freight rates. In the evening he had held a meeting at the school and practically nobody had turned up. The day John Firth, the Conservative candidate, had come the hall had been packed.

Even when my friend Ian MacInnes, who was the Socialist candidate, had held a pier-head meeting there had been plenty of people who had come to ask him questions so that he nearly missed the steamer which was to take him on to the next island.

'We will knock Jo off his perch this time,' they had all said; but when the count was made his majority was even higher and his position more impregnable. Although there was an interregnum when a Conservative represented the islands, the Liberal tradition is deep seated. With each successive election all the old grievances are given a thorough airing and the ground is pawed over angrily, but in the end it is the mistrust of change which prevails.

Although the tendency is to resist change, there are changes which are taking place. When I had first returned to the Island, my immediate impression was that it had remained exactly as it had been and was all the better for it. In fact this is not so. The changes are there all right and they are far-reaching ones.

For example, the islands are becoming less insular. It is a process which has started within each island. When I was a boy our own Island was, as I have remarked, divided against itself, one end against the other and if the rivalry was friendly it was none the less real. But it went further than that. By and large all the islanders were staunch Presbyterians but there were no less than five churches on the Island, so that there was not even communal worship. The same thing applied to schools. There were little schools dotted all over the Island each serving a small part of it so that each succeeding generation had no conception of community life as a whole. Now that has all altered. There is a fine central church and a splendid modern school attended by all the children on the Island so that they are brought together in one unit with its own prides and prejudices. This breaking down of barriers has gone further. It is true that the north isles still view their south neighbours with suspicion but they are beginning to realise that they have problems in common and that they are stronger if they stand united. The day is surely not far off when the links between north and south will become stronger and not so bedevilled with petty jealousies and suspicions. As I write, there is already talk of an inter-island air service, which would be a big step towards bringing them closer together. At present it is impossible for a north islander to visit Kirkwall without having to spend at least one night away from home.

There are other changes too. On the way north we had stopped off to take a cup of tea with Eric Linklater whose fame as a

174

writer is great and who returns every year to visit his native isl-s. I asked him if he had noticed much change over the years. He said that, as a child, he remembered them as brown islands but that each year when he saw them again they seemed to him to be becoming greener and greener. It is, of course, true, for cultivation is becoming more and more intense and yearly more hill land is being claimed by the farmers.

The farmers are in fact in the forefront of change for there is no resistance to new ideas and new methods. It is their willingness to introduce mechanisation on their farms which accounts in part for the depopulation of the islands, for machines replace manpower and young men finding no employment leave for well-paid factory jobs in the south. This depopulation of the islands is what causes the sociologists their greatest concern but it is also the symptom of a more favourable trend. With improved methods both in farming and fishing, the islands are getting richer. Over the ten years from 1951 to 1961, according to a letter in the *Orcadian* by the Vice-Convener of the County Council, the population of the north isles fell by 22 per cent. During the same period the *per capita* exports rose by 43.6 per cent. A fine example to set the rest of the country in productivity. The main concern is that the level of population should not fall below the level required to maintain community life. An ablebodied man lost to a piece of machinery is a potential father of a family lost to the community and it is the children who will be required to carry on the traditions of sturdy good husbandry for which the islanders have always been noted throughout their history.

Is it too much to believe that the time will come in the not too distant future when a drift back to the islands will begin. Living space is becoming in shorter and shorter supply in the south, wages are high but the cost of living is becoming always higher so that people are constantly working harder for less real reward. Already the price of houses and land in the more remote corners of Scotland is going up as more and more people seek an escape from the pressures of an industrialised life. Perhaps they will one day think of taking the step across the Pentland Firth to start a renaissance of the half-empty islands. Those who do may be exchanging the new lamps of civilisation for the old but I I do not think that they will find that they have made a bad bargain.

The night before we were due to cross the Pentland Firth and start the long journey south, we had supper with Ian Mac-

Innes at his house up on the hillside overlooking Stromness. Ian is a fine artist and a left-wing Socialist whose controversial letters enliven the correspondence columns of the local Press and earn him the reputation of being something of a firebrand. He is also a genial man with a lively mind and a determination to see better conditions in the islands. He was one of the prime movers in establishing a co-operative movement amongst the fishermen in Stromness to improve the marketing of their fish and find new markets for such by-products as crabs. It is a bold step in the right direction and sets and example which could be followed with advantage in other parts of the islands.

When the time came to leave, Diana and I stood for a moment by the garden gate while our eyes got used to the starlit darkness. Suddenly the whole sky to northward was suffused with light like the distant prospect at night of some big city. Then slim, wavering searchlight beams swept across the heavens, growing brighter and brighter and changing through all the colours of the rainbow before finally dying away. For fully twenty minutes we stood silent while the whole sky erupted again and again in a fantasy of coloured lights. At one moment they would fade to the flicker of a will-o'-the-wisp and the next the whole firmament would blaze up again, as if all the bonfires of a thousand years were throwing their tongues of flame to the sky in one glorious moment of rejoicing.

It was the Merry Dancers – the Northern Lights – telling the story of the sunlight that glittered on the frozen ice-fields of the Polar cap and promising the spring which was sure to come.

As the lights died away the darkness returned for a moment more impenetrable than before and the night was still, save only for the systole and diastole of the sea – the very heartbeat of the great implacable ocean which brings life to the Island and, in its turn, can be such a grim taskmaster.